THE PRACTICAL GENEALOGIST (ANOTHER VIEW)

JAMES STUBBS

THE PRACTICAL GENEALOGIST (ANOTHER VIEW)

Copyright © 2013 by James Stubbs

ISBN-13: 978-1482040845
ISBN-10: 1482040840

Preface

Genealogy is difficult. We read (overwhelmingly) that it's easy. It's not. We read that genealogy is made even easier in this modern day by exciting and new technology. Without the firm use of the old, established, tried and true basics, that's not true either. In sound genealogical research those basics must come first and the technology second. It's the content and not the delivery. We also read that genealogy is fun. It is.

Books and software in the genealogy field have continued to expand. A recent re-examination and updating of the proliferation of available genealogy resources and software programs has prompted the writing of this book. I wanted to put these new developments into context with the field of genealogy as it was practiced in the mid-twentieth century Not only do I remember the nature of the work some sixty years ago, I also remember the excitement when the internet and accompanying promises made of its potential arrived. Overnight, genealogy would become fun and easy. Hundreds and hundreds of websites mushroomed, containing hundreds of millions to billions of names within which could be found our ancestors. Within this "razzle and dazzle" it became apparent there was much redundancy and many, many of the websites (and "how-to" books) contained promises of the same information and results. Their potential is being oversold and there is overkill in marketing.

I don't criticize the importance of the data, but the way it is being "hyped". The expectations of a beginner may be too high. Many of the promised results will be unreachable. In the vast landscape of modern genealogy it's not difficult to find surnames which match those you are looking for. The trick is to find those to whom you are related.

That there is much more data available now, and that it's much more accessible can't be denied, but it still must be thoughtfully searched for. I can remember the initial excitement in reading of the explosion of new tools to be made available to genealogists. The trend is ongoing but my reading of it today is tempered by many years of putting it to the test. None of this is meant to disparage the work. Genealogy remains extremely interesting, exciting, fun, and rewarding, and though challenging, pays high dividends.

Table of Contents

The Setting (The Way It Was)

When I began my research some sixty years ago, genealogy was quiet, measured, and challenging. Those who delved into it were very serious and dedicated but you had to visit an archive or a library which had a genealogy section to find them. In the information age of today you don't have to go very far to find a widespread buzz of genealogy. Genealogy had little commercial implications then and vital statistics documents were obtainable from cities, counties, states, federal agencies, and courts at a small cost. Obtaining these documents for your files today must be budgeted as there is a significant cost of doing the work (not requiring certified copies will save money). Genealogy today is big business (an industry, actually).

Bypassing genealogy 101 at this point (it will come later) I will merely say that I was extremely fortunate to have had access to important information from my grandparents' families. Both of my grandfathers lived for a dozen years after I began the work and were responsible for giving me a very good start.

The very nature of genealogical research calls for its being "spread out". It calls for a workspace that fits that description. Ideally, kitchen tables, dining room tables, living room floors, and walls or corkboards can be put to good use when putting together pieces of the puzzle. Genealogy is a field based on relationships, and relationships are more easily visualized when their elements (components) are tangible and can be handled, moved around, stacked, re-arranged, and actually laid out (by hand) in various patterns of pedigree charts and family group sheets.

When I look at a laptop sitting on a desk or table it's amazing to me how much data it holds. However, there can develop a strong sense of detachment (a disconnect) between the data and the researcher. The "spread out" phase is missing and it's this concept which is missing in the laptop. It's the "analog" characteristic of the former which is the source of hands-on references found in this book.

There are plenty of areas today which are pursued because the technology is exciting and is at the center. In genealogical research proper it's the content and not the delivery system which should be of prime importance. There are some very good analogies, music and stereo equipment being among the best. Digital stereo of today (speakers, receivers, amplifiers, mobile devices, etc.) delivers a "cold" sound. It lacks the distinctive warmth of the vinyl LPs and tube amplifiers of yesterday. Both of the latter are analog, but truer to the sound they're reproducing. Kodachrome slides from SLR cameras of fifty years ago have a certain warmth not found in the digital pictures of today. The sound of many cellular phones is terrible (digital, but terrible). Many news reports, interviews, commentaries, book promos, etc., originate from cell phones. Distortion is common. Some are mostly undecipherable when listened to.

Perhaps the most easily seen or heard demonstrations of these cases in point are singers appearing on TV, in concerts, in clubs, and in movies, or heard on CD's, tapes, and records. The industry uses the word "enhanced" to describe the sound. The word should be "altered" (falsified, exaggerated). We have no idea of what the voice actually sounds like. Technology can amplify the voice, which is useful, but it can also manufacture a voice, which is deceitful. This goes back to a previous theme. Responsible use of technology (new tools) results in great improvement in many activities, and irresponsible use of technology results in deception. Genealogy benefits from the proper use of tools employed in the practice of sound fundamentals and is damaged by their improper use.

It could be said that genealogies which were put together on the desks and tables which were always present in the libraries, archives, and courthouses of yesteryear, have a "warmth" not found on those derived from ahnentafels, attachments, websites, GEDCOMS, and data merges, etc., of today. The former give a stronger sense of familiarity derived from a "hands-on" approach used when putting them together.

I was in my public library yesterday. The main room was full of computers (several dozen, all being used). I doubt that all of those library computers were being used for purposes usually thought to be associated with libraries. There was not one patron table or desk to be found in the entire library. The old desks and long tables of the past were inviting and much more suited to library work. The world of "new age" technology is a sterile one and in genealogy can cause you to lose touch with the very ancestors you're looking for. The author is an apologist for keeping the tried, true, and proven theory and practice at the forefront of genealogical research. The new tools can be useful but aren't the be-all and end-all of the work.

Sixty years ago was a different time, a very different time. It was the beginning of the Korean War but not too far removed from the end of World War II that all of the remnants of pre-war America had been washed away. The contrast between 1950 and now are striking but it didn't happen overnight. There has been change in just about every facet of our lives.

I could begin with baseball. In the 1930's and '40's professionals played because they loved the game. There wasn't much money in it. There were baseball heroes but no celebrities. They were accessible. If you stood outside of a locker room after a game there wasn't one player who would walk by you if you wanted an autograph on a program or baseball card. The season was of reasonable length. It was a summer game and wasn't played in the freezes of early spring or in heavy frosts of early autumn. Much of the above persisted into the 1950's.

Today the seasons of the four major sports are overly long and generously overlap one another. Playoffs extend the conflict further and it's deliberate. No time to review a past season or contemplate the next one.

In former times there were grocery stores, butcher shops, green grocers, bakeries, and drug stores. Now there are supermarkets, pharmacy chains, Walmarts, Targets, and discount chains, and each carries almost complete lines of everything. Self-serve produce stands and meat lockers in the supermarkets are loaded with vegetables and cuts of meat but those who stock them aren't green grocers or butchers. It's an "assembly-line" world.

Cereal shelves seem endless and most product boxes are gigantic with little choice in sizes. Some of the staples of the past are still there but are overwhelmed by the new "innovative combos" which keep coming. It's all about packaging and marketing.

Radio of yesterday was something to be looked forward to. It was quiet and entertaining, and was listened to by all, especially in the evenings. Commercials were infrequent and non-intrusive when compared to today's rapid-fire blasts which occur in frequent "hard breaks" (can be as many as 4-7 spots in a row in my market). Radio broadcasts of the past were relaxing and entertaining in stark contrast to the "hyper" programming of today.

If your telephone rang sixty years ago it was for you or someone in your family. Today is the day of "caller ID boxes" and unwanted calls outnumber personal calls.

Hordes of new technological goods and services are being thrown at activities and problems of today resulting in a watering down or obscuring of quality solutions.

Movies were a major diversion in pre-war America, during World War II, and after. Movie theaters were rather elaborate, the screens were large, and there was no feeling of claustrophobia. It would probably take a month or so of major house releases of the past to equal the number of weekly movie releases of today. The large theaters have been torn down and replaced with multiple "pill-boxes" where a dozen or so movies can be shown at once. The many new releases of today are needed to fill the "projection-room" theater complexes with movie-goers. The increase in quantity has been accompanied by a decrease in quality.

These examples weren't carefully chosen to illustrate a point, but were random ones which came to mind. Taken together they identify a trend and other activities chosen would strengthen the trend. When compared to the times of sixty years ago life today is frenetic. Its components have been multiplied and amplified. More is better is its theme. It has spawned a tidal wave of acceleration.

The point is that one would have to be naïve to believe that genealogy hasn't been caught up in the transition. It has. Genealogy requires focus and doesn't lend itself to a fast pace. Having hundreds and hundreds of millions and billions and billions of names to sort through doesn't make it easier, as is implied in much of what we read and hear. Good genealogy is "custom-made".

In the school year of 1950-51 I began taking graduate classes in geology and was teaching undergraduate geology labs at Columbia University. These years, and those that followed, were my early years in doing genealogy. In those days most of the research was done on site, through correspondence, or by telephone. I was very fortunate to be living in two of the top sites for genealogy (New York City in the winter and Washington, D.C. in the summer). Several of my experiences will illustrate the state of the work in the 1950's and will introduce a central theme of the book.

As a teaching assistant at Columbia I had access to the vast resources of the university, two of which provided a huge step up in my beginnings in genealogy. First, my staff ID allowed me into the seemingly endless stacks of the highly endowed university library (Low Memorial). Second, the university map room was superb and opened up to me the three major areas of my research (the U.S., the U.K., and Germany).

To my surprise, the stacks held many, many more books than the library shelves and were a treasure trove of reference material (and collections) from a wide range of categories. Masters and doctorate theses were filed by subject or department. Some rare items and collections were under lock and key but could be signed for and obtained from a librarian. They couldn't leave the library and memory tells me, they couldn't leave the stacks. Without elaborating further, you can imagine the volume of resources held in those stacks which would benefit the genealogist. I was at Columbia for two years. I roamed the library and its stacks pursuing my geology degree and looking for material for the labs I taught. I also took advantage of those exceptional facilities to build a foundation for the genealogy work ahead.

The other resource was the map room, heavily used by those involved in geology. Local, regional, and nationwide maps (and gazetteers) of the United States can be easily found in this country with a little bit of digging. It was in my foreign lines that the map room at Columbia came into play. One of the heirlooms which had been passed on to me was a rather small German Prayer Book (Reformed) which contained a two page inscription by my great-great-grandmother. She had written down the villages and landmarks of her parents' birth.

I was in the map room one morning looking for these places on World War II aerial photos of Germany (complete coverage) taken by the Army Air Corps. Translations I had obtained of my ancestor's inscription (in "Old German") gave the village names as "Sunschine am (on) Steinsberg" and "Stetten". The extensive locator indexes for the photos revealed no "Sunchines" and five "Stettens". While involved in my search, Dr.Walter Bucher, a renowned German Professor of structural geology, came into the room. "Mr. Stubbs, what are you looking for?" I showed him my notes and he became interested. "Sunschine is not a German word but it sounds familiar." After a short pause, "it's Sinsheim, in the area where I did my master's thesis!" He quickly found it on the photos, "Sinsheim" located on the "Steinberg" river. Nine miles to the southeast was "Stetten".

Dr. Bucher showed me how to write to the Burgermeisters (mayors) of the two villages and I received letters from the Pastors of the Reformed Church in each village (the mayors had forwarded my letters of inquiry to the Pastors). Each letter contained genealogies (certified with the Pastor's seal) of direct family lines.

In addition to the two resources at Columbia, the third New York City Resource was the genealogy section at the imposing main branch of the New York City Public Library in downtown Manhattan. It was a very large section, self-contained in a spacious room with a very high ceiling and many levels of bookshelves lining the walls. It was at once attractive and utilitarian. There were many tables on the main floor surrounded by extensive card files, more bookshelves, and a central librarians' counter. The genealogy section was several times larger than my county branch library building of today (one of the larger ones). It was open, bright, and inviting, and I haven't forgotten it to this day. A great place to spread out and do research, and only a subway ride from Columbia.

I didn't know it at the time, but the genealogy section of Manhattan's main library branch was a fore-runner of genealogy facilities which would spring up in libraries all across the country in the decades to follow.

There were many stops in Washington, D.C. for genealogists, and while I was on the East Coast I took advantage of the top three, the National Archives, the Library of Congress and the D.A.R. Library (Daughters of the American Revolution). Because the business of government goes on inside and the records of the nation reside within their walls, government buildings in Washington are massive. The architecture is historic and impressive. I spent my six years of college summers driving a cab in and around Washington and never stopped being in awe when in the presence of the buildings housing our national government. The D.A.R. Library was imposing in its own right and had different criteria for patron use than the government sites.

The National Archives and the Library of Congress welcomed patrons and visitors and both had ample reading desks on which to work. The main reading room of the Congressional Library was huge and filled the main floor beneath the library's large rotunda. There were some bookshelves in the reading room which contained often-used or generic volumes. Most of the material sought by patrons (or members of Congress) would come from the endless stacks filling the out-of-sight reaches of the building. Index card files took up most of the reading room and it was from these that one would fill out request slips to take to the main desk. The desk was large and circular, following the form of the rotunda above. Many reading desks (many dozens) surrounded the main desk, all in circular rows interrupted by aisles for access. The reading desks were a dream. Individual desks, each with its own reading light. They were numbered, but in spite of that, you had to carefully mark where you had come from when you left your desk, or it would take some doing to find it when you returned.

The reading room(s) in the National Archives Building was entirely different. There were very large, long, and high reading tables, running almost the full length of the room. As with all good reading desks or tables, they were slanted toward the reader. The tables were set up in pairs, were facing each other (back to back), and the reading stations were defined by high ("kitchen counter") chairs stationed down the rows. The tables were large because the census schedules (enumerator sheets) were quite large.

Two things about the procedure surprised me a great deal: one, the fact that we were checking out sets of original schedules filled out by the census takers in the homes (they made three copies of each sheet) and two, the very large size of the sheets. They were bound in correspondingly large hard-cover books which were signed for and checked out at a desk at the end of the room. Request slips were handed in at the desk and clerks brought the books out to the patrons (one binder at a time). I still remember (vividly) turning the pages of those large schedules filled out some hundred years before by the enumerators! There's really no basis for comparison between the original census records I was privileged to work with sixty years ago and what we see today on the microfilm readers in the archives and libraries throughout the country, or on the web pages we see on our computers. The contrast can't be properly addressed.

The third site in Washington was the D.A.R. Library, located in the Headquarters of The Daughters of The American Revolution. It is situated virtually on The National Mall and is only two blocks from the White House. The D.A.R. Library had one of the largest genealogical collections in the country and one could say that its main reason for being was genealogy. It was spacious, had plenty of tables for research, and many freestanding bookshelves as well as many more along the walls. I remember it as being a long room with its length being a main feature of my first impression. The library had two sections, one for the general public and one for D.A. R. members. The members' section wasn't restricted to stacks but was a separate library. In addition to a comprehensive reference collection (found in the general public section) the members-only section contained thousands (upon thousands) of researched and vetted genealogies. I remember that non-member patrons could use the members' section if accompanied by a member or carried a "letter of introduction" from a member giving permission to look at their file.

In those days the D.A.R. Library differed from most every other library in the country having a genealogy section. It contained genealogies (thousands)! The other libraries had book collections (some quite large) which contained reference books particularly specific to genealogical research and were highly valued by the genealogist. The genealogies available were published and there were very, very few due to the cost. There is little doubt that the D.A.R. Library was far and away the site of the largest collection of individual genealogies in the country. Because they were the passports to D.A.R. membership and were carefully researched and reviewed, they were most likely the most reliable group of genealogies available. I suspect that's still true today.

While commuting between New York City (winter) and Washington, D.C. (summer) I took advantage of a third resource available in the East, situated between the two. It was the Friends Historical Society Library at Swarthmore College in Philadelphia. Many of my immigrating English ancestors of the late 1600's and early 1700's were Quakers and the library at Swarthmore had the largest collection of church and historical records of the Society of Friends in the U.S. I took the train down for a weekend (Pennsylvania RR) and filled two spiral notebooks with notes. I have in my files a hotel receipt for $2.50/night which I consider to be a strong sign of the times.

In the pursuit of ancestors in the 1950's, location was every-thing (no internet, no webpages, no e-mail, no social media, and very few how-to books). However, being on the ground in a facility of primary sources was unmatched at the time, and remains so today.

The Journey

"The journey" in this book comprises the last sixty years. There has been a natural and predictable increase in the field of genealogy as new sources and resources have become available. Access to these has increased dramatically. Genealogy has been one of many areas in which the development of new tools and technologies has changed our lives. As the years of "the journey" have gone by, millions of people have taken up genealogy for various reasons. Ancestry.com, the largest (by far) of the commercial websites, claimed two million paid subscriptions in July of 2012. The history of genealogy through the period is revealing. It was interesting to experience and is still pertinent to the present-day genealogist.

I should go back to my first exposure to genealogy in the 1930's, some 20 years before "the journey", when I began "doing" genealogy. I was in what we called grade school, and I didn't recognize that what was going on was genealogy (I'd never heard the word), and was unhappy about being involved. During summer vacation-time my maternal grandparents took trips to visit their siblings on their farms in Indiana. I loved being on the farms and looked forward to the trips. Although I didn't hear the word as a young boy, my grandmother was a genealogist. On the way to and from the farms we stopped frequently in small towns along the way while my grandmother went into courthouses to inquire about family names or into drugstores to check the phone books. My grandfather and I sat in the car while my grandmother was on her quest and I didn't like the stops or the waiting. I wanted to get to the farms or back home to play. Many years later when I inherited a box of her handwritten notes on scraps of paper or envelopes, which she had made during those small town visits, I was reminded of what "hands-on" genealogy really is.

The evolution of the field of genealogy (or is the word revolution?) was slow, steady, and orderly in the early years, later to be interrupted by several landmark events which changed its status overnight. The earliest of the resources for genealogists that I remember was Everton Publishers, Inc. out of Logan, Utah. Their "Genealogical Helper Magazine" began as a small publication but was an early leader for many years. I read it in the '50's and 60's but found it less useful than their "Handybook for Genealogists" which came later. The handybook contained detailed data from all of the nation's counties by state. It was invaluable for writing or calling county offices for vital records. The department or court where a particular record was kept was spelled out (it varied county by county). Addresses and phone numbers were among the listings. The latest handybook I have is the eighth edition published in 1991. It is a substantial hardcover book. The latest Handybook I find reference to is the eleventh edition (revised 2006). Everton Publishers developed an online presence but was eclipsed by the "Cyndi's Lists" and "DearMYRTLES" of the day. The business was sold in 2004.

With the emergence of self-publishing, surname forums, many new or expanded local, county, and state genealogical and historical societies, and many, many new topical websites,

the numbers of published genealogies have increased significantly. Their value depends entirely upon their quality. Increased access to millions upon millions of civil and
ecclesiastical vital records via microfilm, microfiche, and the
internet, has been a catalyst in the process.

Several websites came into being which extensively listed
and linked to genealogy-related how-to books, data bases,
periodicals, and articles or lessons etc., from many sources, all
found on various and newly emerged websites (and other
resources) covering the subject. "Cyndi's List" (Cyndi Howells)
and "DearMYRTLE" (Pat Richley-Erickson) were the front-
runners in this group. The years of 1995 and 1996 were the years
when these two significant websites came online (1996 for the
former and 1995 for the latter). "DearMYRTLE" began a long
series of columns on genealogy-related subjects and "Cyndi's
List" became the most comprehensive online genealogy directo-
ry available. The latest versions of "Cyndi's List" contained an
updated tally of resources listed and they soon reached into the
thousands and beyond. The pace of the awakening to genealogy
in that period could be gauged by her latest list. The tally in
recent versions of today number close to three hundred thousand!

There were, of course, organizations which pre-date "the
journey" which influenced genealogical research in the country.
Three prominent ones which were there in the early days of the
movement were The New England Historic Genealogical
Society (1848), The Daughters of The American Revolution, or
D.A.R. (1890), and The Genealogical Society of Utah, an arm of

the LDS Church (1894). They all have (and had at the time) extensive libraries.

The (very) late 1980's and all through the 1990's was the age when commercial ISP's made their appearance and genealogy websites soon followed. It was a time of rapid growth, but in the early days AOL (America-on-Line) dominated the field in both categories. AOL was the king of the mass mailers. Hardly a week went by without an AOL disc falling on the doormat. Each contained an offer of free online minutes and each succeeding offer exceeded the last. AOL founded "Genealogy Forum", a (the) leading internet resource at the time. AOL wasn't a very good ISP but many genealogists subscribed to gain access to the "Forum" which had important features available to AOL members only.

The history of genealogy and its growing importance in the world (which occurred during "the journey") can be measured by the changes which took place in public libraries across the country. I have mentioned the 1950 genealogy section of the Manhattan (main) branch of the NYC Public Library System as being a portent of what was to come. In the ensuing decades I have seen the genealogy sections in city and suburban libraries change before my eyes.

During my working years I spent quite a bit of time downtown in the business district of the city where I lived. The main branch of the city libraries was an important resource for my business and I used it frequently. When I had the time I would search the shelves for books that could have a bearing on the genealogy projects I was working on at the time. There was a large checkout and return desk inside the front door and several reference desks scattered across the main floor. Among the fewer reference desks on the second floor was one in a very far corner of the library, and served sections of bookshelves relating to some of the more obscure subjects (like genealogy). It was never very busy. At the time my local county library branch had perhaps several dozen books that might have a bearing on genealogical research.

Moving ahead in time, the old status quo has been reversed. The big change in which the way that genealogy was viewed occurred in the late 70's and early 80's, and today the downtown library has a substantial genealogy section. It is served by two side-by-side reference desks, which are often manned by two genealogy librarians during peak hours. Each desk has a phone wired with a library extension for the department. At noon, early evenings, and weekends there were waiting lines to see a librarian and incoming calls were put on long holds. Calls from home or the office for a quick look-up were most often met with busy signals (a far different world than in the early days of "the journey"). The genealogy department (in keeping with the rest of the library) had plenty of work tables and copy machines. Books and photocopies could be spread out, analyzed, and sorted on site.

My branch library now has a respectable genealogy section. As local genealogy societies have grown and prospered they have acquired and built up their own libraries until a place to store them becomes a problem. Our branch library has agreed to store the local society library, much of which can be found on bookshelves in the reading rooms. Many society books can be checked out as those belonging to the library. Until they were removed due to lack of space during remodeling, there were two large showcases in the library just inside of the front door. Several times a year, extensive genealogy exhibits appeared in these showcases with a calendar of meetings and contact details of the local society.

I have evidence of the period of the awakening of genealogical awareness in my files. After their genealogy collections had been significantly built up, comprehensive booklets on genealogy and the respective genealogy divisions of the two library systems I use, were printed and distributed at the libraries. There is no publication date on the city library system booklet, but the county system booklet dates were 1990, 1992, 1994, and 1997, and were published in cooperation with the local genealogical society. They both appeared at about the same time and were very useful resources.

Unfortunately, as with many new and rapidly growing endeavors, scams popped up and genealogy had its share. The most widespread was another period of mass mailing, but in this case each mailing was addressed to a specific individual. Surnames were the key to the scam. The offer was to provide you with the origin of your surname, a genealogy of "your" ancestors (very generic genealogy), and often enclosed a crest or coat of arms or included one in the offer. I didn't make note but I think that the cost of the offers was in the $19.95 to $29.95 range.

The novice genealogist, or those who contemplated becoming one, were the obvious targets of these offers. The genealogies and coats of arms were for the most part legitimate, but could be easily found in encyclopedias or in the reference section of most libraries in the country. The likelihood of one of these unsolicited genealogies or coats of arms being tied into your particular line was remote. The mailings persisted for several years and the enclosures were often rather elaborate, and I suspect the mailings met with some success.

A word that comes to my mind as being characteristic of the latter years of "the journey" is "speed!". Highly praised by many, it's a word that is not necessarily beneficial to every activity. Genealogical research is one to which it is not. At this writing, the "hot" branch of technological advances (where the battles for supremacy are taking place) is in mobile devices. Mobility is another expression of speed (which I've addressed) and I can't see where mobility would have serious application in the field of genealogy.

In summarizing six decades of history there are bound to be highlights and landmarks, and there were. In addition to the usual day-by-day movement which occurs in any field, there were some further events and highlights which should be mentioned, along with three "striking" milestones, which marked the progression of genealogy as it moved through "the journey". Each of the three had a major impact upon the process.

In 1976 Alex Haley published a book called "Roots" which was a novel based on the life of his immigrant ancestor who was brought to America as a slave in the late 1700's. In 1977 ABC Television broadcast a television mini-series ("Roots"), taken from Haley's novel and for the twelve weeks it ran it was a blockbuster and sparked a wave of public interest in genealogy. It seemed that all of America wanted to find their immigrant ancestor. I was working in a genealogy library at the time as a volunteer and witnessed the crush. In 1979 a sequel of "Roots" was broadcast on ABC. It was titled "Roots: The Next Genera-tion", was shorter in length, and brought the story up to con-temporary times where an actor played the part of the author, Alex Haley. The sequel was shorter in length, and wasn't as well received, nor did it have the same impact as the first.

In 1978 there was another event that ultimately had a long term effect on genealogy because of what it developed into. It was unheralded at the time and won't be included in my three milestones. I have a newspaper clipping from my hometown paper's center section dated June 16, 1978 that depicts the period following the broadcast of the first "Roots" mini-series. The dateline was Pittsburgh (UPI):

"Genealogists, who have made their search for "roots" one of the three most popular hobbies, have received an exciting new aid. The world's largest genealogical library has been linked to hundreds of local outlets. The Mormon genealogical library has 1.5 billion pages of vital statistics microfilmed from all over the world...

Nearly 300 local wards (parishes) across the country are now hooked up with the Salt Lake City facility". The article contin-ues with a statement from Church spokesman Jerry Cahill who said that "after the television movie 'Roots', usage of the Salt Lake City library more than doubled from 2000 researchers a day to 4200". He said that spot checks indicate a similar increase at branch libraries and that the church is budgeting to add 30 to 50 more of the libraries each year in meeting houses all over the world.

Thirty-four years later (2012) the Church gives the figure as 4500 facilities and the former branch libraries have been re-named Family History Centers.

The next two landmarks of "the journey" (following "Roots") deal with the Genealogy Society of Utah/LDS Church Library and its successors. I think it's safe to say that at the beginning of the "the journey" (the last sixty years) members of the LDS Church (Mormons) were, as a group, proportionately more involved in genealogy than the general population. If that is still true, and it may be, it's to a lesser degree than in the 1950's (or in previous times). The searching out of ancestors who have gone before is a basic tenet of Mormonism and the LDS have been an important segment in the field of genealogy since the late 1800's.

In 1894 The Genealogy Society of Utah was organized. In 1944 it became The Genealogy Society of The Church of Jesus Christ of Latter-day Saints. In 1976 the name was changed to The Genealogy Department and in 1987 came the most signifi-cant name change of all. The new name was The Family History Department, by which it is still known today. In contrast, their library has had but two names, The Genealogy Society of Utah Library (1894) and The Family History Library (1987). As you enter the library, the original name appears on the left outside wall, and the present name appears on the right wall. Overnight, the word "genealogy" was replaced by "family history" in church manuals, forms, magazines, correspondence, and TV and radio spots. The same thing occurred in classes, meetings, and conferences.

Interestingly, because the LDS Church and its library had been major players in the field of genealogy for such a long period, much of the genealogy world followed suit. Genealogy became family history. I don't know the reason for the change but I suspect that the reason was because the term family history seems more user-friendly and less intimidating to church members than the word genealogy. Of further interest (and significance) is the fact that family history isn't genealogy, but an adjunct to it. History is a series of chronological events. Genealogy (beginnings, origins, genesis) is the study of pedigrees and descendancies. History, by its nature, moves forward. Genealogy, by its nature, moves backwards.

Relationships are prime in genealogy. We work with vital records (name, birth or christening, marriage, children, and death) because it is by these that all of us are identified. To establish or verify, we have to be absolutely sure that we are dealing with the right people. This is another of those areas in which technology and seemingly inexhaustible data can complicate things and this becomes more of a problem at the end of "the journey" than at its beginning. Modern technology in all quarters has side effects and genealogy has its share. This should always be borne in mind when doing the work. Having said all that, hardware and software have given genealogy a big boost. A highlight in my journey was the purchase of my first computer and printer just over twenty years ago. I bought them specifically for genealogy and their usefulness exceeded expectations. The computer is an absolutely marvelous word-processor and printers eliminate many trips to Office Depot. Immediate choice of fonts and font sizes gives far greater flexibility.

A very important segment of the genealogy community apparently hasn't made the change to "family history" from "genealogy". City, county, state, and national genealogy (or genealogical) societies have retained the original (and proper) term to describe their purpose. There may be exceptions but they must be very few.

The third (and memorable) landmark of "the journey" took place in 1999 when the LDS Church rolled out its website, FamilySearch.org. In 1998 the church had adopted a new program named FamilySearch, which included Ancestral File, International Genealogical Index (IGI), Family History Library Catalog (FHLC), and Personal Ancestral File (PAF). The release of these programs on the new website caused quite a stir. Finally, the vast resources of the Salt Lake City library would be largely available online. I remember announcements (online and offline) which amounted to a countdown to the launch. There were a few postponements but the day finally arrived. Lines allocated to the website at the library were hopelessly swamped and overloaded as the amount of traffic was sorely underestimated. Many technicians were brought in to add lines and a reasonable balance was achieved (it took weeks).

In the early days the time that a user was allowed to stay online was allocated (10 or 15 minutes, extended to 30 as lines were added). When your time was up you were simply cut off. If you wished you could re-enter the large group of people waiting to get in and repeat the process all over again. After several weeks plus, many more lines had been added, traffic subsided somewhat, more sections of the library were brought online, and the operation settled in at a more normal pace. From the beginning, early mornings and late evenings were best.

There was great anticipation of the arrival of FamilySearch.org. That particular library had been a mecca for genealogists for decades and it was a destination for many excursions (field trips) by genealogy societies and other groups. Many similar trips were taken by individuals, myself being one of them. With so many resources at our fingertips today it's difficult to remember (thirteen years on) what it meant at the time to have access to the LDS library.

Another development (a fairly recent one) is the use of DNA codes in genealogical research. It has been used in forensics and the determination of paternity for some time but now has opened up the new field of genetic genealogy. It might be termed a biological advance (as opposed to technological) and holds much promise for the future. Common in its applications of today is in seeking out unknown relatives (the closer the match, the closer the relationship) and in determining which of the early pre-historic groups a person belongs to. Genetic genealogy can only grow with time as more individuals are added to the database. Through DNA, origins and migratory routes in historic times have been tracked and confirmed, and its science has much to say about migrations that took place as man moved out of Africa and began populating the other continents in the earliest of days. A fascinating field!

I remember the 1990's as being a time of a rapid increase in genealogy paid internet "start-ups". Most were quite small by today's standards but had genealogies and books exclusive to their sites. Fees were in cash or "in-kind" (exchange for credit). The inevitable "shake-out" occurred in which most of the sites were merged or purchased. There are two giant online genealogy sites today, one paid site and one free site. The paid site is Ancestry.com (1997), a spin-off of Ancestry Magazine (no longer published). The free site is the LDS FamilySearch.org,

My previous reference to genealogy becoming big business during "the journey" was confirmed in October 2012 when a group of investors led by London-based Permira Advisors agreed to purchase the Ancestry.com genealogy website for $1.6 billion (reportedly, there will be lawsuits by the shareholders). There are indications that the new owners will be aggressive. In the last two months (November and December, 2012) I've heard national radio commercials on stations in several states advertizing a "tryancestry.com" website. They aren't radio "spots" but are rather detailed commercials. In the ads Ancestry claims 11 billion documents in their databases.

In November 2012 yet another (unexpected) genealogical outreach appeared that illustrated the broad exposure the field of genealogy receives. The "American Philatelic Society" is stamp collecting and postal history group of 34,000 members. Despite the name it is an international organization with members in 110 countries. Its November monthly journal cover was a montage of family photographs, an 1877 British envelope (cover) mailed from Ellesmere (U.K.) to Philadelphia, and several enlarged images of postage stamps. The cover title was "Family, Philately, Genealogy" in script.

Inside was a six- page article entitled "Using Genealogy Resources for Philatelic Research". On the fourth page of the article was a comprehensive paragraph on the LDS "Family History Library" in Salt Lake City and its branch library system, confirming the high visibility of that particular genealogy resource. There was also a picture of patrons working on computers in one of the branch libraries (no work tables in sight).

There has been a natural and predictable increase in the subject of genealogy as new sources and resources have become available. Access to these has increased dramatically. Genealogy has been one of many areas in which the development of new tools and technologies has changed our lives. If a new activity, venture, hobby, pastime, endeavor, or pursuit catches on, sooner or later it will show up on TV. Genealogy is no exception. Apart from the novel "Roots", which took a more conventional route from a book to a television miniseries, there are three TV shows dealing with genealogy in its own right. One was scholarly and the other two are in the category of what I would term reality shows. All three held my interest.

In 1997 PBS and KBYU (Provo, Utah) produced a TV series called "Ancestors". It contained 23 episodes and was a good video primer for genealogy. The other two shows were on the current (2012) prime time schedule prior to summer recess. "Who Do You Think You Are?", a TV series on NBC, was a "knock-off" of a show on the BBC in the U.K. It ran to 27 episodes in two and a half years and was cancelled by NBC in 2012. "Finding Your Roots" is a TV series on PBS with an identical theme. They were both genealogy-related and both traced the ancestry of celebrities or well-known personalities far into the past. In order to appeal to the general public, each series deliberately drew from the lives and heritage of well-known people and the format was successful.

There is, however, a caveat for viewers and especially for those doing genealogy (a caution for which reminders have and will appear in the book). The stories of the guests on these shows are far from the norm. I would guess that researchers for the shows spent more of their time and money searching for subjects whose legitimate genealogies could be traced back through the centuries, than was spent in putting together the genealogies themselves. The quality, completeness, and preservation of the records found are far from the norm. Only those who have searched for ancestors will know how rare they are. It looks too easy and it is. That's a word that I don't remember having heard associated with genealogy at the beginning of "the journey". At its end, genealogy and the words easy, easier, and easiest, are frequent companions (misleading, in my view).

The Hands-on Approach

A term which has nearly come into disuse, "hands-on", is rarely heard today. However, most people understand its meaning, and it has a distinct application in genealogy. "Hands-on" doesn't necessarily mean handwritten or manuscript, although there will be some. "Hands-on" means personal involvement. Both the term and practice had wide use in the early days of "the journey", and its demise can be tracked through time. Automation and other technologies are the cause. Automation is the enemy of "hands-on".

Life is different. Many situations and things which were an important part of the "hands-on" era haven't been experienced or aren't remembered by many (if not most) people today. Painting with a broad brush, simple examples would include telephone conversations or discussions with city, county, state, or federal departments and agencies (or churches), telephone answers by phone, give and take, shopping in stores (offline), hard copy papers and files, meetings, classes, real Christmas trees, choirs, checkbooks, finding a knowledgeable clerk or associate in a place of business, actual storefronts, a phone answered by another person, and genuine Q&A's, etc. I would place all of these in the "hands-on" category and many are rare today.

An absolutely vital side of "hands-on" is accessibility. You must have access to your sources and resources. Large workspaces are important for proper layouts and modeling. You're dealing with life-size files, papers, forms, charts, and diagrams, etc. You're dealing with the actual, not the virtual. There are benefits from working with the real thing. Initial impressions (or first glances) can be important. Computer-generated genealogies have a "cold" look (which puts me off). "Hands-on" work sheets and charts are easily recognized and have a certain "warmth" about them, and personally, I tend to give them more credence. Graphics workups are more easily achieved "hands-on". In today's environment the latter approach is more difficult to accomplish, but is well worth considering.

For the non-genealogist (or those contemplating "delving into"), a real-life "hands-on" approach and accessibility (or loss thereof) in genealogy can be demonstrated by analogy. I've always been a strong believer in analogies and one follows.

Nobody wants to be in touch with the IRS but sometimes it's important. The contrast between its operations at the outset of "the journey" and the present is sharp. Many will be surprised at the IRS operations of the 1950's and 1960's, but the transition from accessibility to being inaccessible through the years mirrors many other experiences.

At the beginning of "the journey" you could dial up the IRS and talk to an agent (there were plenty manning the phones). There were neighborhood IRS offices where you could pick up forms, file your returns, ask your questions, have your filled-in forms checked by an agent (or even filled in by an agent as you furnished your information!). Tax day has always been an important one (the last day of filing without a penalty). In 1955 it was changed from March 15th to April 15th. Postmarks on returns are important. For many years (on either date) many, if not most, post offices had a postal employee at the curb until midnight, taking return envelopes from filers as they drove by. Today there are very, very few post offices where you can file after closing hours. In those days it was a "hands-on" exercise for the taxpayer. The returns were guaranteed to be postmarked on tax day. At the busiest post offices the lines of cars were several blocks long. Tax day night was "a happening". Those were the "hands-on" days of filing taxes. Those were the days of IRS (and post office) accessibility. If all of this seems silly, you might keep in mind that "hands-on" filing is more secure.

When compared with an "I remember when" list, the disconnect in today's world is obvious. How long has it been since you were able to talk to an IRS agent by phone (without an appointment or a "call back")? How long has it been since you've been able to walk into a local IRS office with your paper work? There's a specific counterpart to the IRS story as it relates to genealogy.

When I started doing research I could pick up a phone and have 10-15 minute conversations with county clerks and recorders, entity archive departments, probate courts, church offices, reference librarians (a most helpful and patient group), or sextons etc., all essential to genealogical research. Now most are isolated from the public. Today is the era of "leave a message and we'll get back to you", or "contact us by e-mail and we'll respond in the order in which they are received". On many websites the "contact us" button may list several options but a phone number is often (and deliberately) missing. We live at a time of widespread social contact, but one of "arms-length" and inaccessibility that extends far beyond genealogy.

Research and development (R&D) of mobile devices is the big item in technology today and new versions are released in increasingly shorter intervals. "On the move" is the current lifestyle (and style of business) for both the calling party and the called, e-mailed, texted, or twittered party. Genealogy benefits little from the age of mobility because the parties called are usually in buildings of entities and their departments which have been stationary for a very long time. The need for "on the run" genealogy seems limited.

The British have a long-standing affinity for genealogy. It's been an important element in their culture because the Monarchy is dependent upon it. In addition to the Royal Family, British Nobility and Aristocracy pay particular attention to it because of the succession of heirs. Interest in genealogy in Britain runs high and the national involvement with genealogy has been much more far-reaching than it is in America. They have much more genealogy than we because it runs many centuries beyond ours in North America. During "the journey" the broad gap in national interest between our two countries began to lessen, principally because of the milestones along the way.

In my files I have a 1937 special number edition (a soft cover coffee-table book of 72 pages) celebrating the Coronation of King George VI of England (KGVI). He was the father of Queen Elizabeth II (QEII), the present Queen. On page 17 of the book is a genealogical chart of the kings and Queens of England running from Egbert (802-839) to King George VI (1936-), a year before his coronation. Egbert's reign began nine hundred and eighty-seven years before George Washington's presidency. That helps put genealogical things into perspective. Your perspective will change as you do the work.

In late February of 1989 I traveled to England for a trade show. The day before it opened I took a London cab over to the venue to check on the preparations. During the trip, the cab driver noticed my accent and asked if I was an American, and then asked about what had brought me to London. I told him about the trade show and added that I had set aside another day to look for my ancestral village of Eldersfield up in Worcestershire, 100 miles to the northwest. He asked me if I did genealogy and I replied that I did a lot of genealogy. Without a word, he pulled over to the curb, turned off the meter, and began to tell me about the genealogy club he belonged to.

From what he told me, it was a good club, of a good size, and met bi-weekly (more often than most genealogical societies meet over here). They were to meet that week and he invited me to attend. I couldn't because of a meeting. We chatted for about 10-15 minutes and the emphasis was on his wanting to make sure that I could get any help I needed on English genealogy while I was in London. He gave me his card and wrote down the time and address of the meeting and the name and phone number of the club president. He said I could call anytime and she would be happy to answer my questions. I thought the situation was a good anecdotal example of the English interest in genealogy. Have you heard of an American cab driver pulling off the road and turning off the meter to have a conversation with a passenger?

After the trade show I stayed in England another day and took a train north to Cheltenham where I hired a cab by the hour to take me out to the remote village of Eldersfield. It's my ancestral home. Thomas Stubbs was christened there (c.1692) and he is my 5th great-grandfather.

The driver had to scout around a bit to find it and when we arrived I had two surprises waiting for me. First, the village was gone (all that remained were two widely separated houses, one with a thatched roof, and a very nicely converted stone cow barn). They were all occupied. Like many English towns and villages, I was told that the inhabitants of Eldersfield dispersed during the plague (1665) to discourage contagion. Many houses were destroyed during the War of the Roses and the British Civil Wars.

My second surprise was an old stone parish church and graveyard which were situated on a rise overlooking the plain below. As I was looking around a high school boy came up the hill to greet me. When I asked if I could see the inside of the church he replied that his grandmother had the key and she would be back in a little while. When she returned she gave me a tour of the church, which still has weekly services. She told me that their "Mother's Sunday" service was on the Sunday before I arrived. The boundaries of Eldersfield were laid out in a charter issued in 972. The church was a Norman Church and has a Norman tower. It was dedicated to St. John the Baptist and was founded in the 1100's. Additions were made through the centuries with the last one being completed in the1600's. Walking around the churchyard you can see where the additions began and ended because of the differences in the stonework.

Grace Paterson (one "t" because it's Scottish) was the grandmother, and about a month after returning home I received a very nice note from her along with a newly printed history of Eldersfield and the church (the return address on the envelope was: "The Old Cow Byre, Church Lane, Eldersfield, Clouscestershire. England". Also enclosed were pictures of the sanctuary (it has a stone floor) showing all of the flowers from "Mother's Sunday". It was a further confirmation as to how people in the U.K. view genealogy. She knew how important all of this would be to a genealogist.

Staying with the British, there's another area which can be used to describe the practice of "hands-on". Some thirty-five years ago I told my genealogy classes that genealogy is like detective work. You're looking for missing persons (or suspects, if you will) and the clues you are using or looking for, and the evidence you are working with, is often no different than those used in police work. Our searches, however, can be made more difficult because the time lines we deal with extend far beyond even the coldest of "cold case files".

It's been said that the British love a good mystery (they do). They have more than a few well-known authors who have written series of short stories or books featuring the same protagonist. This prominent position in the world of literature has carried over into movies and television. I've been a long-time fan of both British movies and television mini-series which fall into the "mysteries" category. They can usually be identified and separated from American works because British writers pay particular attention to detail. My favorites have been the police dramas, most of which have been produced as mini-series. Today I find that they can be used to illustrate the type of "hands-on" research in genealogy that I've advocated. I've used the following mini-series examples (also two movies) because they are readily available to those who would like to look them up. All of the screen plays take place within the time frame of "the journey" and some are quite recent.

The inaugural series of "Masterpiece Theatre" was the BBC's production of "The First Churchills" broadcast on PBS in 1971. In 2008 "Masterpiece Theatre" took on a new format (essentially two titles and two categories, namely "Masterpiece Classic" and "Masterpiece Mystery!"). There is a third category, "Masterpiece Contemporary", which is seldom seen.

Among the subsequent "Mystery!" shows from England are the popular police dramas shown on PBS. Many of the police dramas preceded the new format. Those I've chosen to list are "Prime Suspect", "Inspector Lewis", and "Wallander" ("Prime Suspect" precedes the new format). The "hands-on" scenes in "Inspector Lewis" and "Wallander" are short and are integrated into other phases of the investigations. "Prime Suspect" is set in a large London precinct and the "incident room" scenes are protracted with a large number of detectives in attendance. Episodes of "Inspector Lewis" and "Wallander" which contain short situation room scenes are "The Quality of Mercy" (2010) and "A Generation of Vipers" (2012) for the former, and "The Man Who Smiled" (2010) for the latter. "A Generation of Vipers" has several whiteboard scenes and is a good example. "Prime Suspect I" (1992) has several important "incident room" scenes and they occur throughout the story.

The tie-in with genealogy has to do with the "hands-on" techniques employed in the police investigations depicted in the shows. They are quite applicable in genealogical research. Genealogy work is quite like detective work.

The three shows I use for reference (to illustrate the point) have these situation rooms of one sort or another in the script. The thread is that the work that goes on in these rooms is "hands-on". The tables and walls are covered with papers (stacked and scattered), boxes and folders of evidence and research, pictures, maps, tape, notepads, charts, and in most cases, whiteboards and markers. In complex cases there are large annotations and arrows, maps, blown-up pictures, case summaries, rap sheets, forensic photos and reports, etc., all pinned up or taped onto a wall or whiteboard. Annotations, conclusions and theories are written on the whiteboards or wallboards surrounding the displays. Arrows may be drawn to track the current thinking. With one exception, the situation rooms have a similar look.

The "situation room" in "Wallander" differs from the rest and is simply a long, "busy" table in what appears to be a large, multi-purpose room with high ceilings, which apparently is shared with other personnel. Wallander and his team (five in number) discuss and analyze as they sit around the table, each with a stack of papers or files pertaining to their phase of the investigation. Pertinent papers and files are thrown into the center of the table or passed around as the discussions proceed. An occasional laptop computer is brought in which contains relevant data.

The practice I'm referring to which is depicted in British police dramas is the use of these "hands-on" situation rooms. The term is heard rather frequently these days but always refers to the modern hi-tech situation rooms of TV or government. CNN has an evening news show titled "The Situation Room" which has run for six nights a week since 2006. In literature, "Situation Room" is a book published in Barcelona in English and Spanish (2010). A prominent example of a situation room in the news today is the one in the White House (a high-tech one).

Two movies which should be mentioned and which contain large situation room scenes from different eras are "The Battle of Britain" (British, 1969) and "War Games" (American, 1983). The first movie takes place during WWII and the second during the "Cold War". In military terms the situation rooms would be called operations rooms. A credible British source defines operations rooms as containing a "collection of selected information about a complex and changing situation", and I'm going to throw these movie examples in with the police mini-series situation rooms. Both rooms in the movies belonged to the armed forces of their day and graphically illustrate the divide between the sophisticated and technological situation rooms of today (at the end of "the journey ") and the "hands-on" situation rooms of WWII (very near the beginning of "the journey").

British and German aircraft groups (British fighters and German bombers) are placed across a large board "mock-up" of the European Continent, the English Channel, and Great Britain (largely Southern England). The pieces are moved around the board (plotted) by specialists using "croupier sticks", and their position is based on data being phoned in from British Air Bases and lookouts along the coast. The workers at the board (on the lower level) are Waaf's (Women's Auxiliary Air Force) and on the phones are non-commissioned Royal Air Force men (on the second level surrounding the board). Both groups are without their jackets but are wearing the standard blue shirts and ties. On a third level are officers in full uniform who are in touch with and are responsible for releasing the British Fighter Squadrons.

The situation room in the 1983 movie was at NORAD headquarters (The North American Aerospace Defense Command) and was a huge room. The main wall was covered with many over-sized monitors controlled by dozens of computers on the floor being staffed by air force technicians wearing ties. I don't consider typing on a computer keyboard to be a true "hands-on" operation. The contrast between the two scenes is striking. The "hands-on" military operations (or situation) rooms of World War II would be sadly outdated in today's conflicts, but the use of similar "hands-on" techniques in today's genealogy would not be (as is the case in modern police work). The key element of situation rooms is the display and the use of them would greatly benefit genealogical research.

I favor a blend of today's technology being utilized for data (vital statistics, transcripts, abstracts, correspondence, and storage, etc.) and "hands-on" files, forms, charts, notes, and "situation room" practices being used for doing summaries and analysis. The latter allows for far more flexibility and you can more easily organize and direct your search.

I've gone to some length to discuss the similarities in doing genealogical research and the work of detectives. I've drawn rather heavily on TV and the movies for the comparison because the TV and movies are there to be seen and everybody is familiar with them. This section and the cited TV and movie references have two purposes. The "hands-on" sequences in these shows are meant to give a glimpse of what a modern "hands-on" investigation (or research project) would look like. A second purpose is to remind that "hands-on" isn't obsolete!

For my own part I have had long years of both "hands-on" experience and bringing in technologies as they became available. I'm a geologist by profession and my specialty was oil and natural gas. Much of my exploration and development work in the office was of a situation room variety. The situation rooms were offices and conference rooms. The major elements of the "hands-on" work areas were 7-foot drafting tables and cork walls and pushpins. The data worked with included electric logs, well completion cards, sample descriptions from wells, and subsurface or topographic maps, etc. The arranging and re-arranging, and adding and removing of these components was essential to the process.

There were many components to the research I was doing in geology and there are many components in the work we do in genealogy, and they lend themselves to very similar treatment. I read many lists and indexes of available (new and old) resources available in the genealogy field. To reiterate, it's all technology, speed, and ease. Not a word about "hands-on" with the exception of how to avoid it. The data we deal with in genealogy seems endless. In my view, we should take advantage of every way available to unravel it.

In my geology office, x-sections, structure and stratigraphic maps, e-logs and correlation lines, oil field maps, etc., were laid out on drafting tables and walls. I also had similar (or identical) suites of data on microfiche, computer monitors, the internet, and projectors. Working with the larger scale data on drafting tables and walls had an aspect not found on computer screens. Storing or recording results (data) on computer discs (or microfiche film) is very effective, but doing the work on them is less so. Viewing or working with raw data on a much larger scale gives an entirely different perspective. It's a great way to summarize clues (evidence) and could be called "clues at a glance". There is much to be said for laying out geology on a 7' drafting table, or walking along maps and x-sections mounted on a 25' cork wall. There is also much to be said for laying out genealogy on a whiteboard, or on a kitchen/dining room table, or on the living room floor. When you step back for a look (be it geology or genealogy) there's no additional data but what's there looks different. You can also pull up a chair for an extended look.

On a smaller scale, working with genealogical data "hands-on" is similar to doing geology on the larger scale. It provides the opportunity to manually stack, shift, and sort the names, files, charts, forms, places, dates, and vital statistics. I've carried my office practices over into genealogy and they work just fine. We all have our own systems, but whatever system we use, "hands-on" will contribute and should be tried. Don't deny yourself the opportunity to spread out your work.

I've shown that important phases of geological research benefit from the visual. I've shown that important phases of investigative police work benefit from the visual. The same holds true for genealogy. There are a great variety of pedigree charts available, and you should choose carefully the ones you use. The best ones are graphic and "clean". They chart relationships between people and the peoples' names should pop out at you. The names tend to be buried in the additional data on the newer four-generation charts I have found the old LDS five- generation legal-size charts to be the best, though the letter-size four-generation charts are the most widely-used today.

My genealogy "bible" is an 8-generation pedigree chart that I began in the early years of "the journey". It's folded so it can fit into my files and the folds have been reinforced many times through the years. Going back in time on the chart, the vertical spaces between ancestors of each generation become less (grow smaller) and there are fewer of their vital statistics shown. In the earliest two generations there are just names. In twelve of my lines I go back to the 9th and 10th generations and I've turned the chart over and roughed out the extensions on the back.

There are more than a few lines that have taken years to push back just one generation. In areas where I'm working and the information on the chart is sparse, I can pull out a five-generation chart from my files to work from. Of course there are gaps (some quite large), but the "bible" shows me where I've been, where I am, and points to where I'm going. I come back to the 8-generation chart time after time because it puts my genealogy and its status into context. It's a "genealogy at a glance" tool and gives a picture as no other. There's nothing comparable in my files.

I have mentioned that each person should have a system which suits their particular program. These chapters largely reflect mine. I am very fortunate to have a good set-up. I have a desktop and a laptop computer, both of which have my genealogy file installed. One is a Mac and the other a Windows machine and they have different genealogy software (for different purposes) supported by their respective operating systems. My hard copy files are kept in two four-drawer legal file cabinets. There is a 22' U-shaped, chest-high, "dry bar" in the basement that is indispensable for laying out working files in use at the time.

I have a whiteboard and markers for displaying and "trying out" ideas. The dining room table is confiscated when a surface of its shape and size is needed. I'm also prone to pulling out large-size copy-paper sheets (11 x17) to sketch out possible names, relationships, dates, and places (an additional site for "trying out" ideas).

I take my laptop with me when I go to the archives, libraries, or meetings. I use it as a reference. I don't make entries to my files while I'm out, but record the research in notebooks or on note sheets. When it's been worked through at home and verified, it goes onto the computers. If it remains a work in progress it goes back into the file cabinets. The on-site research notes are strictly "hands-on".

The Myth of Sharing

I read dozens of ads and promotions for genealogy software (although it's usually called family history software these days). In the descriptions, reviews, and listings of these products' features, there is almost always a strong reminder that they are particularly suited for sharing. Ease of sharing is an important aspect of the new technology that is being promoted today. I have the same reaction to these sharing features as I had to the constant reminders that we now have millions and millions (let alone billions!) of names to work with. The implication in each instance is that it will make things much easier. It probably won't. "If it's too good to be true it probably isn't".

In the early days of "the journey" the sharing and exchange of genealogical information took place in correspondence similar to that used in personal and business contacts. It wasn't the avalanche of data promoted to be easily shared today. Any new information, whether yours or someone else's, must be checked and absorbed before being added to your genealogy. If bad research (or names) makes its way into your genealogy it is contaminating and will be very hard to remove. If you've carefully built up your genealogies with solid family groups and pedigrees, you will have a feel for the authenticity of what's been worked up on the same lines. "Caveat emptor".

Genealogies (genealogical research, to be specific) are proprietary. They belong to you and you are entitled to do with them what you wish. It's your work, and you can share them, put them on family forums, publish them, send them out to relatives (borders on an obligation), expose them to the social media, or keep them to yourself. There is, however, an important ethical qualification. If there are living persons included in a genealogy, it should not be shared or distributed without their permission. This brings up a very important point. At the start of "the journey", and through most of the years I've been doing genealogy, there were no computers, no internet, no e-mail, no cell phones, no social media, and very little identity theft. Today we are surrounded (almost overwhelmed) by all of them. When you release your data today it goes everywhere (and quickly). Conversely, when incorrect (or bad) information becomes publicly available it is widely distributed, and goes on forever. It was always a good idea to guard your information (personal or otherwise) but now it's essential. It's a dangerous world out there.

There are areas where sharing can be very beneficial and others where it is not. I've found that genealogies on file at genealogical and historical societies, or those worked up by their staffs, are of higher quality and generally safer (but still at risk). Queries or submissions on lines listed in society journals can be useful. Postings (yours or others) on the many forums should be considered but handled at arm's length. I've had some experience with sharing, none of which involved the new software. A few were satisfying and one resulted in a breakthrough. There were more that were frustrating or unpleasant. The practice should be carefully considered.

My first example isn't sharing in the sense that is being advertised today. I include it to separate it from the sharing that is being widely promoted. It illustrates a very basic tenet of genealogy that is essential to good work. The principle is that your genealogy begins with you and with your family.

Sixty years ago (at "the journey's" beginning), I received a letter from the wife of a second cousin as a follow-up to a dinner in New Orleans when we all first became acquainted. The letter contained information on my grandfather's (and her husband's father's) family, and mentioned some further notes her husband had in his possession. Many years later (after she and her husband had died) I came across her letter in my files. I knew they had one daughter (an only child) whom I located through her father's obituary. She had the family papers and pictures passed down from her mother. In our first correspondence she put me in touch with another second cousin who was doing genealogy. Each of us had records, letters, and pictures from siblings in the family (our ancestors) that we exchanged to fill in some gaps. It was a very memorable experience and resulted in the reuniting of records and pictures that had been in separate branches of our family for many years.

In 1998 I returned to working on a long-standing "brick-wall" in my paternal grandfather's line, stemming from his maternal grandfather and grandmother's names (his first and her last). My grandfather lived for ten years after I began "the journey" and we discussed ancestral families many times. As I began working on the line I had trouble confirming Squire for the husband's first name and Bowyer for the wife's surname.

There were good family records (and memories) of the family and little doubt in my mind that the names he gave me were correct. I had worked my way through my pedigree chart and had reached the specific line and generation of my grandfather's maternal great-grandparents (my third-great-grandparents). My grandfather had names for both. The husband's first name was Squire and his wife's name was Nancy (nee Bowyer). One of the most traditionally challenging chores of doing genealogy is searching for a wife's family name.

One of Squire's sons, Stephen, was my grandfather's grandfather, and he disappeared from a town bridge during high water in 1848, leaving a wife and five children. As I worked up this family I found no convincing evidence that Squire was the husband's first name and not a description of his status, nor that Bowyer had been his wife's family name. I was reminded many times by my sources that squire can be a form of address or a title (I knew that). There have been many squires whose names were Robert, James, or John, etc. As I researched Squire's line I was able to follow the family through two coastal states, and down into Ohio. There were three Squires and three Stephens in several generations (confirming that Squire was a family name) but I was unable to sort them out from the resources available.

There were Bowyers in the county and I worked through all of the families and determined that Nancy wasn't related to any of them. Having confidence in family tradition passed down by my grandfather, I pressed on. The whole story can be an extended one, but a shortened version brings out some useful points, and demonstrates the two sides of sharing.

I'm a long time member of the genealogical society of the Ohio county where Squire and Nancy lived (and raised their family) and the society maintains an extensive file of surnames that members are working on. From 1998 to 2001, I periodically sent in my latest data and pedigree charts, including some of my recent theses sketched out on 11x17 sheets. At that point, Squire's line was lagging far behind on my pedigree chart and I decided to concentrate my genealogy efforts on it exclusively until it was resolved.

In 2003 came the breakthrough (two years into my big push on Squire's line). In December 2003 I received an e-mail from a lady who lived in an adjacent state who had also been working on Squire's line in Ohio (our two states were over a thousand miles from Ohio). The county genealogical society had sent her a copy of my pedigree chart they had on file. From the chart she thought that our lines might cross and included some of her work. When I looked at her sending I realized that our lines did cross and I mailed off the highlights of my "push" years. One of her direct ancestors was a sibling to Squire and she had spent "30-35" years working on the line. She was a veteran genealogist and her notes (and style) were exceptional. She was 99 years old and turned 100 during our correspondence. I was happy to have information to forward that she didn't have.

She furnished the missing piece of the puzzle by suggesting that I look up a certain Deed Abstract in a fourth state that I hadn't considered as there was no mention of it in my years of research. The missing piece was the new state (she also gave me the county). The deed abstract involved an estate and referred to a "Squire and his wife Nancy" (of Ohio) as heir and legasee (sic) to the estate. I wrote to the county for a copy of the deceased's will and created a beautiful family group sheet of the father and mother and their four sons and six married daughters. I had searched for and found Squire's family in three states, but nothing I had come up with pointed to the fourth (the one with the answers).

I knew which of the three states that Nancy had been born in but hadn't found proof of her family name. I also knew that there were often several ways of spelling the same name (Pierce/Pearce), but I hadn't considered the alternate spelling that appeared in the probate records or the Deed Abstract. It was the same name and was pronounced the same, but was subject to two spellings. At the end of the quest, when I finally had some answers, I wrote a 2500 word "white paper" on Squire's family and sent it out to my family and fellow genealogists I had been in contact with during the process. Lastly, and very importantly, the unfolding of this odyssey reveals the crucial role of locality. Genealogists know this.

As I begin the section on the other side of sharing (the frustrating and unpleasant side), I'm able to use a continuation of the story of further research on Nancy's newly found family name. With a copy of the will of Nancy's father in hand, I was able to push back the line another generation. I posted a condensed version of the family (with Nancy as a child) on the Family Forum, giving the name of their county and state, and requesting further information on the line. I received an answer from a lady who thought we might be working on the same family and if we were she had data on the family of Nancy's mother (another line new to me), and would share what she had. I sent out what I had from the will and Deed Abstract and heard back that it was the same family and she would send out what she had. Several weeks later I received another e-mail saying that her data wasn't well organized and she didn't want to send it out in its present state but would do so later. That was eight years ago and I've heard nothing since. I don't regret sending out what I had (it was all useful information) but am disappointed in missing out on what she had on the family of Nancy's mother.

Some years before the Squire and Nancy story I experienced another disappointment similar to the sequel of theirs. The LDS Church has been in the genealogy business (figuratively speaking) for a long, long, time and the genealogy operation has evolved into more than a few departments and has many facets. Most of the facets are designated by their acronyms, IGI (formerly CFI), TIB, MCC, FGRA, FHL, and PAF, etc., and many are trademarked. These are mostly databases and indexes of submitted records from many sources, and also include data from church extraction programs. In some instances the name and address of submitters can be retrieved.

Early in "the journey" I found a primary source record of an 1819 marriage of one of my great-great-grandfathers in Ohio. As I worked this line on the LDS website I found the same record on one of the databases, along with the name and address of the submitter. The record was on a database that could only be added to by a relative of the bride or groom, which would mean that the submitter and I were (distant) cousins. I had spent a good deal of time getting to the point of the marriage and had some good information on the groom's family. I had found the family name of the wife but hadn't gone beyond. There were many families and individuals in the county with her family name and I hadn't been able to single out her father within the group. Since my "internet cousin" had also found the marriage record I had hoped that he might have been able to take the wife's line back further.

I wrote a letter to the submitter asking if he had more information on the line and where I might find it. I included enough of my genealogy to prove that the bride and groom were my direct ancestors. I was careful not to ask for his work but only for direction. I heard nothing for a few weeks and wrote a second letter, adding that perhaps my first letter had not reached him. Both letters had my return address on the outside of the envelopes and neither was returned. It was a disappointment not to hear. In 1991 the LDS Church announced that the names of submitters, patrons, and sources would no longer be available. Perhaps others had experiences similar to mine. That was the same year that a new system was introduced for turning in names to be processed by the Church.

I have found that the reality of sharing (or attempting to) doesn't live up to the hype. Even if you don't choose to share or have nothing that would help, a simple acknowledgement of an inquiry is appropriate. When you begin to correspond, share, or exchange, your genealogical research takes on a different dimension. Putting posts or inquiries on forums or message boards is a beginning to sharing. It's not a person-to-person sharing relationship but it is sharing, and is an invitation for others to share.

In the course of business there have always been "bubbles" in the business cycle. In the context of this discussion a "bubble" is a grossly over-extension of a good thing. It has been referred to as a "bubble" because it bursts. The buildup is usually artificially fueled, is characterized by a proliferation of startups, and it ends in a crash. Most industries have had "bubbles". Among the most memorable (or notorious) are the stock markets (multiple), the oil and gas industry (OPEC oil embargo), savings and loans, the railroads, the airlines, the .coms, the ISP's, television (cable and satellite), telephones (breakup of AT&T), and housing (sub-prime mortgages).

There was a genealogy "bubble", but unless you were involved in genealogy, you probably missed it. A sharp increase in the interest in genealogy began in the late 1970's and the start of the "bubble" began a few years later. Someone had discovered that money could be made in the field of genealogy and a predictable flurry of startups occurred. I remember most of the activity to have been online but there were also new magazines, books, CD-roms, and newsletters. There was much advertizing and many schemes as the new "industry" players attempted to acquire and assemble their own commercial databases. I was somewhat amused (but not very) that some websites offered to buy databases and compiled genealogies through cash offers, discounts on services, exchange (their data for yours), or other incentives, while others offered to include your data on their site for a fee.

There was a database scramble for some years until that side of the genealogy "bubble" burst, followed by a "post-bubble" shakeout. Most of the new enterprises disappeared through purchases, mergers, or going out of business, leaving only the big players. The interest in genealogy hasn't waned and I believe that an overextension of products (a "bubble") still exists, apparently being centered in offerings of new software, of which the majority include features for sharing. If you partic- ipate, it would be well to keep in mind the workings (and history) of the social media. Once you send it out it ceases to be yours.

Our family was unwillingly caught up in one of the database building schemes. One of my wife's sisters was the designated genealogist for the family and she worked on or oversaw a compilation of the family's genealogy. The project extended for over several decades and resulted in a three-volume set of the family genealogy. My wife's sister sought professional assis- tance for difficult sections of the U.S. lines and contracted out the foreign language lines in Europe. Family members provided their own personal histories and the publication date was 1996. There were some thirty copies printed and distribution was to several generations of family members.

Some time later I was working some websites online and be- gan to see familiar localities and names (including my wife's and mine!). They were pages from a published genealogy of my wife's family. I was stunned when I saw it and even more stunned when I saw how complete it was. My wife's family genealogy was on a commercial database that had a scheme for the public to buy or earn data from their site. It was something like ten or fifteen cents a page to download from their site, but for every ten pages of sheets and charts you sent in, you received a free page to download. The familiar people and places on the site took up a large section and included many family group sheets and pedigree charts. I took out copies of our books for comparison and the online pages (page after page) were copies (scans?), and not transcriptions. The group records and charts were exact duplicates of what I was looking at in the books. The three volumes combined exceeded seven hundred pages of text, charts, and pictures. I'm only in the family by marriage, and yet my name appeared on five pages of the online book version.

The information contained in the books was gathered for and distributed to family members and was not intended for general release. This particular website published the names of submitters and in this case it was a couple who lived in a state where some family members lived but the compiler wasn't one of them. At several family reunions following the book's release on the website I asked if any of the attendees knew the submitters. My wife asked others by phone, and we didn't find anyone who knew the submitters. All of the family members weren't contacted (it's a large family).

There were some serious ethical violations here. The books could have been stolen, but the fact that the couple's names appeared as submitters makes that less likely, but they may not have known that their names would be published. The books may have been loaned or borrowed. However obtained, a knowledgeable and responsible genealogist (or person) wouldn't have put the contents on the internet without permission of the family and individuals involved. As to motivation, the submitters would have received over seventy pages of free downloads from the commercial data base company, and I suspect that was the answer.

We read and hear about how genealogy brings families together (all sweetness and light). It's true but not the whole story, and we hear it mostly from those who are selling genealogy software. Genealogy isn't all sweetness and light. Many families are divided. When you do genealogy you get a good dose of reality. Some genealogies are done with imagination (they're imaginary). Second or third husbands (or wives) are left out by the compiler because the compiler didn't like them (it happens). Children are omitted from family group records for the same reason (it happens). Criminals and saints alike belong on family group sheets. To be a responsible genealogist you must be objective. Leave the editorializing to family history.

In some families, records vital to genealogy are not released to other relatives or branches of the family. There is no response to letters, phone calls, etc. (as in my story of the 1819 Ohio marriage in which there was no response from the submitter). The same happens in closer families. It can be very demoralizing to work up a family genealogy that contains gaps in data that you know exists, but is held by estranged family members.

I have read a lot in the genealogy world (offline and online), but there's little (or no) mention of a downside. Most of the downside occurs in the area of genealogy that we call sharing.

The Lowering of the Bar

The lower standards of what is acceptable today in our society is ongoing. The new reality is all around us but may not be noticed by many. Not to single out genealogy in the process, but it is a part of it, and must be included in any discussion of "lowering the bar". Younger people won't remember or have heard about much of what is in the book, but it's important to bring out the contrasts that have come into play. They may not know that they have never heard what the actual voice of their favorite singer sounds like through his or her concerts and CDs, or appearances on TV, radio, or in the movies ("enhanced" sound is the reason). They may not remember when Olympic swimmers put on their swimwear, dove into the water and swam, instead of donning swimsuits of special design and fabric, and wearing hi-tech goggles to cut down resistance as they cut through the water. They may not remember when news anchors read the news and didn't sit around a desk and chat. Technology is responsible for many of the contrasts between "then and now". In genealogy we must be wary of technology over content (substance).

Since the subject of this book is genealogy, its place in these contrasts (deterioration of standards) is examined in detail (although one would hope that it needn't be). "The setting" (the way things were), and "the journey" (sixty years of genealogy) have been discussed and we now have arrived at present status.

It's not what I would have predicted or imagined. Standards have been relaxed, and in most instances, in very obvious ways.

In high school, college, and graduate school there are prerequisite courses, and in most professions, certification of some sort. There is also a preferred track in genealogy and to jump ahead can bring discouragement and disappointment. There will always be pressure from the marketers. Two key words in their world appear to be fast and effortless. There is no such thing as an effortless genealogy (unless it's inherited). In the heyday of the new genealogy.coms, I remember one that offered a "starter kit". The trouble with most starter kits is that they contain items that you aren't ready for (or may never be needed in your way of doing things). It would be better to start off with a few simple necessities such as spiral notebooks (or steno pads), pedigree charts, and family group sheets. I can see starter kits for home aquariums, but in genealogy I'd go a la carte.

A feature of hi-tech genealogy is the "rush-to-publish". It's the "rush" part that can be damaging. There is material in your working files (some of it the result of much research) that is not ready for publication. Tie up the loose ends before putting it out. We must learn to recognize the superficial. There is good work available and we should seek it out, but among the good are the "whipped-up" versions. A bona fide, indisputable, primary source record is a prize to a genealogist and when one is found I've seen it appear over and over again on forums and message boards, having been pounced on by submitters. The practice isn't limited to individual records. In working through lines on the internet it's not uncommon to see identical genealogies appear from different individuals. It's impossible to determine who did the original work unless there's a comment or complaint on a message board. Redundancy doesn't help in research but there's much of it from the "rush-to publish" faction.

Sources must be evaluated. It's a critical stage of research. A gauge I've used for a long time with newspapers, magazines, books, television, radio, and the internet has been very helpful. There are certain topics dealing with our work or avocations of which we have acquired considerable knowledge. Sooner or later many of our usual reading material will touch on them and we have an excellent opportunity to judge the source. If the treatment of a subject that I'm familiar with is incorrect (or poorly done) it makes me suspicious of their treatment of subjects in other areas. It's a good criterion to apply.

The same technique will apply in genealogical research. It makes a good yardstick. In the course of your research you will work your way through many compiled genealogies and theories looking for lines that coincide with or cross yours (that's the purpose of a search). If you've been thorough in your work you can judge the usefulness of the information you're looking at. You will also be looking for extensions of your lines and for new lines that branch out from yours. This will all be new but can be evaluated by the quality of the sections of which you have knowledge. Remember that vital records and transcripts won't be altered but submitted material can be (and often is). I have found that the ratio of good to bad is about the same for traditionally published genealogies as for those found on the internet. The situation in either case isn't encouraging. There has been a vast increase in the amount of accessible vital records data and transcripts made available during "the journey". Take advantage of it.

Another indicator of the bar being lowered is in the facilities available to work in. There's a decrease in suitable library facilities available (computers are pushing out the tables of yesteryear). It's a personal view, but I much prefer to do the "nuts and bolts" of genealogy out of books (when available) being used on desks or tables. I prefer "work stations" and note-taking in conjunction with computers, rather than their use exclusively. I have found that there is very little work space surrounding library or NARA computers (or readers).

While in a library doing research you will be going through the shelves in various sections and (again) will need a place to work. All of this would have been easier through much of "the journey" than it is today. In my files I have a lengthy newspaper article from the 1980's about our downtown city library's extensive genealogy division. There is a picture of its curator sitting at one of those wonderful long library tables, surrounded by books from the shelves. He's holding a large, opened, genealogy book. It reminded me of the prevalent "hands-on" research of the day.

Genealogical research is a science and you will learn and use multiple disciplines in doing it (local, national, and world history, geography, land transactions, wills and probate, kinships, wars, plagues, religions, and major migrations, etc.). Your search will take you beyond the genealogy collections in the libraries and beyond the genealogy websites on the internet. Ignoring, avoiding, downplaying, or "lowering the bar" in these associated areas won't help in the results (just the opposite).

There are several segments of the genealogy community that are holding their ground and not "lowering the bar". I would cite public libraries and genealogical (or historical) societies. Before the milestones of "the journey" occurred there were several hundred genealogical societies in the country. This has grown to over five thousand. They are largely volunteer organizations and have retained high standards. Their resources and sources are reliable and they are well-worth seeking out or joining. Their scope ranges from local (county), to state, regional, and national, and one or more will certainly match the localities in which you are working. Although there may be some, I haven't found one that has dropped or replaced the word "genealogy" in its title. Public libraries and their research librarians across the country have a similar approach.

I was in on the rapid growth of genealogy on the internet from its early times, and have been involved since. I've observed a general decline of quality in the field (on and off the internet) although quantity has increased. I can't specifically account for it but it's been more obvious since genealogy has become so popular and since the web has become so active. I think it's more than a coincidence. There are many new people involved in genealogy without any background, nor have they taken the time to acquire it. The correspondence, postings, e-mails, sharing and exchanges of information, articles and reviews, etc., which have crossed my desk are indicative of the decline.

When I post on a forum or message board I am very explicit about what information I have, or what I am looking for. I have received the vaguest of responses ("do you have anything on the Smith Family?"). I have received queries about families with different surnames and from different centuries than my posts. I simply reply in one sentence that I don't have anything that will help. A novice doesn't need to hear a condescending or smart reply.

The transition of the LDS Church's treatment of their genealogy program during the period of "the journey" is of interest. There is a "before and after" air about this chapter of the book, but it's been enlarged to include "before, during, and after". Since the LDS "FamilySearch.org" website is so widely used, and the LDS genealogy program is universally recognized (and influential), and is representative of the period, it is worth examining in more detail. However, there are caveats for church members and non-members alike. There have been changes and amplifications in the program through the years and the process can be considered as a microcosm of this chapter's title. Early changes in the PAF software (personal ancestral file) and the Church's subsequent internet site were covered on the "DearMYRTLE" and"Cyndi's List" internet sites. Later changes are found at "lds.org" and in Church publications and manuals.

There are extensive (and very useful) databases at FamilySearch.org that are available to the general public and Church members. There is a section that is available to Church members only (entries that deal with living persons and personal data). The members making entries in that password-protected section are supposed to be the only ones to have access to their data but it doesn't always work that way. All of the databases are added to and worked with by eligible persons who register. Most of the names and families submitted by members are destined for temple sessions and must meet criteria set by the Church. The standards (or their implementation) for submissions to the Church have evolved through the years and have been relaxed. Following the appearance of FamilySearch.org, I have done a lot of work on its public pages, and in my research lines. The quality of the submitted genealogies has been largely disappointing.

I knew an LDS neighbor who had found a direct ancestor (a great-great grandfather?) who appeared on the site eight times with eight different baptismal or christening dates. I know a woman who visited a local Family History Center (branch library) three years ago to review what was in her Church file. There were two entries in error: an entry showing her husband and her as a married couple and her husband as being deceased (he isn't), and another entry showing her husband as a sibling (he isn't). It took the library assistant one and a half hours on the phone to Salt Lake to make the corrections. She doesn't know where the entries came from.

At the heart of LDS genealogy (now family history) is the family (immediate and extended). The first principle of submitting names on the members-only side is that the submitter must be related to his or her entries. This hasn't changed but the quality control has. From 1942 until 1969 members submitted names on family group sheets and pedigree charts and they were cleared by the Church. I have seen family group sheets from that period that have been reviewed by censors using colored pens. Green pens were used by a censor checking names and dates, and blue pens were used by a censor's checking localities (cities, counties, states, etc.).

A letter "C" was written in red pen next to each name that had been cleared. Sheets were returned with instructions to correct the errors marked by the censors, and when corrected, the sheets were to be resubmitted. It was a pretty tight system and when compared with today's practices, it was a very tight system.

The family group sheets used by the Church in that period (1942-1969) were different than those used today. An obvious difference are two fields in which appeared the name and address of the person submitting the sheet, and another for the "heir". The "heir" was the first male family member baptized into the LDS Church in life. The field marked "heir" showed the relationship of the "heir" to the husband and wife. The latter field was located on a section of the family group sheet reserved for Church use only. In 1956 the term "heir" was discontinued and replaced by "family representative". The "family representative" could be a man or a woman but had to be a member of the Church.. The "heir" (or "family representative") and submitter may or may not have been the same person.

Beginning in 1969 members were responsible for clearing their own names and were responsible for the accuracy of the work. Unfortunately this invites duplication. It also leads to inaccuracies. This change in the method of clearing names coincided with the computerization of entries. When FamilySearch.org came on line I spent many hours on the site reviewing my genealogies and searching for new lines. There was more duplication and more errors than I would have liked. I found marriages that didn't exist and one in which a grandmother was married to a grandson. I found family groups containing a member who lived in a different century. These were the extremes but there was too much of it. There was also good work also but I had to be familiar with the lines to find it .

The original 1969 system has evolved and is still being revised, but all have retained the important element of members clearing their own names. Emphasis on computerization of data and new avenues to sharing are features of all of the newer programs. Yet another release is being readied.

The evolution of parameters that LDS members were to use in submitting names to the Church (destined for the temples) can be easily traced and documented through the "Member's Guides" published through the years of "the journey". The policy of members submitting names only of persons to whom they are related has remained constant (though perhaps not in practice). The guides have all reflected the family relationship policy up until the latest one (2009).

In the section of that guide that covers determining "which names to submit" there are the usual categories of immediate family members, direct ancestors, collateral lines (aunts and uncles, etc.), your own descendants, and biological, adoptive, and foster family lines connected to your family (sounds a bit different). Added to the above are categories that are very surprising:

"Possible ancestors, meaning individuals who have a probable family relationship that cannot be verified because the records are inadequate, such as those who have the same last name and resided in the same area as your known ancestors."

"You may submit the names of individuals with whom you shared a friendship. This is an exception to the general rule that members should not submit names of individuals to whom they are not related".

The latter criteria are very liberal and were apparently too much so. In April of this year (2012) the Church Leaders sent an e-mail to "Registered Users of New.FamilySearch.org". It reminded members that "our preeminent obligation is to seek out and identify our own ancestors" and that the names submitted to the Church should be related to the submitter. This was not a new policy but a reiteration of long-standing policy, and it was to be read in services and meetings in all the wards of the Church. Apparently, the Mormons are addressing "the lowering of the bar" issue.

The heart of the Mormon genealogy program has been the Genealogical Society of Utah Library (now the Family History Library) in Salt Lake City. It was founded in 1894. It has seen many changes and in 1944 the society ceased being a public organization and became a Church corporation. The groundbreaking for the new building was held in 1983 and the present library opened in 1985. Just two years later the name was changed to the Family History Library to coincide with the new Family History Department (formerly the Genealogical Department) of the Church.

Before the name change (which was one of our landmarks in "the journey" chapter) the Family History Centers of today were Branch Libraries of the library in Salt Lake City. As is the case today, they were staffed by volunteer workers and one person was appointed to be the branch librarian (a Church member). The appointed person in charge of today's Family History Centers is the director (a Church member). The other volunteer staffs come from the Church or the community.

There are thousands of Family History Centers in many countries but most are in the U.S. They vary significantly in resources and facilities depending on the size of the congregation (ward), the buildings in which they are situated, and the priorities of the local leaders. The system is again in transition as the Church adds large regional centers and libraries such as the Los Angeles Family History Library and the Riverton (Utah) FamilySearch Library. The former is a more traditional library with extensive book, film, fiche, and map collections and the latter is a computer-only facility. The Riverton Library houses 127 desktop computers in the main room and 24 laptops in a large training room. There is a limited collection of general research books.

In the 1970's I did some very useful genealogy work in one of the LDS Branch Libraries near my home. It was an exceptional example of the system and you could tell when you walked in that it was obviously a high priority of the local leaders. A proper space for its purpose had been requisitioned and remodeled. There were easily accessible file cabinets for films and fiche and built-in bookcases from floor to ceiling for the book collection (hundreds of volumes). A typical library half-ladder was available to reach the upper shelves. The reading room contained four to six library-size tables for the patrons to work on. The lighting was good and a dozen or so researchers could easily be accommodated.

A dutch door (or stable door) with a counter on the lower half separated the office from the main library. Films and fiche coming from or going back to Salt Lake were kept in the office and checked out to patrons for use in the library. Books in the stacks were available for browsing and removing for use at the tables. It was not a circulating facility and nothing left the library.

Twenty-seven years later I paid a visit to the church to see the library where I had done those years of research and was surprised (and saddened) to see that it had lost its pride-of-place status. Its former allotted space had been halved (at least) and chopped up for other uses. The main room was L-shaped with four computers jammed in. There were no work tables and no work areas between computers. Computer chairs on opposite walls bumped into each other when pushed back. Files, films, fiche, a reader, and books (very few) were stored in closet-sized room. It was quite the reverse of twenty-seven years ago and another demonstration of the "lowering of the bar". I hope that the reference books that were once there found a good home as it takes some time to build a good book collection.

In the '80's and 90's I made a half-dozen trips to the Family History Library in Salt Lake City. They were out-of-state trips and lasted for several days each. It's an immense library system and well worth a visit. I spent my time on the U.S./Canada floor where there were a huge number of shelved local, state, regional, and national reference books and family genealogies. A goodly number of staffed reference desks and several dozen long work tables were conveniently located along the stacks. As I recall there were printers and readers in another section of the room. The library always seemed busy. At peak hours you had to wait until a patron left to get a workspace at a table. Close to the entrance and by the reference desks were a few standing computer workstations. The set-up was very conducive to research. Unfortunately, at each successive visit, there were more computers and fewer tables.

I come from a time when it was considered important to know what went on before and this chapter attempts to address that. I also come from a time of briefcases (before computer bags) and my briefcase was my "office". As I moved from meeting to meeting (or library to library), my "office" went with me. My briefcases were rigid with lock or combination. When open, I could work out of them, with file-size divisions and small pockets on the opened top, and more files and accessories in the base. I carried geology reports and maps, calculators, colored ballpoints, triangles, rulers, Prismacolors, slide rules, and genealogy files, forms, and charts. What went in depended upon where I was headed for that day.

I have a computer bag, complete with a shoulder strap (which I never use). I find it far less convenient to work out of, having to pull out several files at a time from the bag to find what I want. I bring out the bag when my computer is a major resource for the trip. To repeat an unfortunate sign of the times, there is often no place to put a briefcase or bag in these new work stations, which consist of a computer only. There's usually no place to put your own computer that you've brought to work with.

The NARA (National Archives) facility I visit occasionally moved into new space some years ago. The old location was smaller but had tables to work off of as you searched for dates, names and localities on the census films. The new rooms have more readers but no tables and I try to get a reader with an idle one next to me so that I can put my computer or notes on the floor by my chair. The bound census indexes are on tables but you need to look through them standing up. It's an unfriendly place, reminiscent of my county library that no longer has any tables (just computers).

A final note on the use of FamilySearch.org. It's from a very creditable source and is well worth mentioning. I've been a member of an excellent county genealogical society for over forty years. I am an out-of-state member since it's many miles from my home, but I have quite a few ancestors who lived in the county. The website and volunteer staff have always pro-vided outstanding help and I have watched it grow through the years of "the journey", along with the increased nationwide interest in genealogy. The society has won many awards.

The current president of the society has worked in various Family History Centers (branch libraries) since 1997 and she has presented more than a few programs on their use. In 2010 the society journal carried comments on such a program from a previous meeting. An excerpt from the journal is a quote from the society president and reads: "www.Familysearch.org is a great site to use and has a wealth of information. It contains both submitted and extracted sources that are included in the various databases of the Mormon Library". She told us "to concentrate on the extracted sources, and to skip over the submitted ones because they may contain errors". Similar comments could be made about other websites but the LDS programs are noted because they are the most visible.

There are extraction programs and there are extraction programs (some are good and some aren't). This might be a good time to differentiate between extracts and abstracts. Simply put, an extract is an exact copy of the contents of a document and an abstract is a summary of what's in a document. The LDS Church has had more than a few of what they label "controlled extraction" programs and they fall into two categories. The first category was begun in 1939 and consisted of one microfilm camera being sent out from Utah to film vital records and registers. This was the only extraction program in effect during the first eleven years of "the journey". This program continues today with 200 cameras operating in over forty-five countries and it remains the best of the lot.

The remaining programs are generally in a "name-extraction" group that have evolved through the years. The first of these began in 1961 and consisted of Genealogical Society employees transcribing names from English parish registers. English parish registers aren't particularly easy to read and this first program of the category was the best of the remaining "name-extraction" programs because it was carried out by staff genealogists trained in the work.

In 1969, the Genealogy Society instituted a computerized system to manage all name submissions and thus was not an extraction program. In 1978, record extractions were turned over to the stakes (regional units). In 1988, a new Family Record extraction program began in which volunteers extracted pre-1970 temple records (for computerization) from their own homes. The extraction path has been from microfilming records (still going on), to parish extractions by professionals in the Salt Lake City Library, and finally to extractions carried out by volunteer church members in various meetinghouses. When working on FamilySearch.org (or the newer ones) it would be helpful to know which program the data you're working with came from.

A New Perspective

Whether you recognize it or not, when you do genealogy you will gain a new perspective. It's a very important word and a second one that should be used in tandem is context. Perspective can be of little help if it's not put into the context of what you're doing or studying. In genealogy there is very little that you're dealing with that's of a contemporary nature. You will be attempting to open up times past (many times past) and each will have its own perspective and context. You must reconstruct the times and places of your ancestors. To retrace their footsteps you must be able to imagine the scenes that those footsteps were traveling through.

One of the first elements you'll have to look at through different glasses is time (not times, or periods, or eras, but time itself). Your view of it will depend upon your age but since you are surrounded by people in all stages of life, the concept of a lifespan (short or long) shouldn't be difficult. Generally, acceptable estimates of a generation are between 20 and 25 years. This range has been workable in my experience. Most of us are working within the last few hundreds of years, and some lines in that range will be difficult (or impossible) at best. The perspective of time can be taken to much higher limits. In my profession I worked with geologic time on a scale which is completely unrelated to contemporary or genealogical time. Ten minutes from my home I drive through road cuts with outcrops of rocks that are 1.7 billion years old.

We learn quite quickly that the number of direct ancestors doubles with each generation. For an exercise in perspective it's interesting to consider a millennium model. Studies have shown that a reasonable probability model would look like the following for someone born in the first third of the 1900's. At the midpoint of the last millennium (1500 A.D., about the time of Columbus) such an individual would have over sixty-five thousand progenitors (direct ancestors) of which about ninety-five percent would be different. Going back three centuries, at the time of the Magna Carta (King John, 1215) there would be over thirty-three million progenitors (mathematically) which was about the population of Europe at the time. Each slot on a pedigree chart has to be filled and it has been estimated that each progenitor would fill about sixteen slots in 1215. That would bring the actual number of progenitors back to two million. Extrapolating these models back to the Norman Conquest (1066) each actual progenitor would fill slightly over one thousand slots on a pedigree chart. These are just models or projections but they give an idea of scope.

Changing (or assuming a different set of) variables from the preceding figures would alter the results by differing amounts, but the pattern is unmistakable and would remain the same. It's inevitable that back in time there will be more slots on a pedigree chart than there were people alive to fill them (assuming that no. 1 on the chart is you or a contemporary). Many will suspect that there will be some duplication on our charts (cousins marrying cousins, etc.) few would suspect just how significant this occurrence actually is over time. It does happen. I have just one progenitor (so far) who appears twice on my pedigree charts and I was surprised when it happened. I hadn't read of the work of demographers who study such things.

One such study which is most memorable to me is by Kenneth Wachter, a Professor of Demography and Statistics at U.C. Berkeley. As stated, it's concise, easy to remember, and (at once) illustrates the concept (principle). Wachter suggests that a post-World War II child born in England in 1947 would be descended from eighty percent of the people living in England in King John's time.

I find these concepts to be fascinating, and they represent a greatly expanded perspective, but they will be of little use in our day-to-day research. Bearing in mind the scope of these probability models and the complexity of going back one thousand years, it would seem that the task of sorting out our ancestors of the last several hundred years would be a pretty tame exercise, but we know that it isn't. It's great fun to theorize on the big picture, but running down the details in our genealogy (even relatively recent ones) can be hard work and quite challenging.

In the realm of perspectives, pedigrees and descendancies should be reviewed. Both are used in genealogical research and a genealogist should become acquainted with their differences. Pedigree charts are the norm, are easy to construct and understand, and are more easily seen to give the answers we're looking for. They are much to be preferred. Descendancy charts come in a variety of forms (layouts) and are often difficult to decipher. They are used extensively when important heirships are involved in situations concerning monarchies, royal families, nobility, aristocracy, Chinese Dynasties, or fortunes, etc. Biblical genealogies are descendancies.

As mentioned earlier, pedigree charts are the road maps that lead us to our direct ancestors. The former are simple and graphic, the latter are cumbersome and often obscure. A case in point. If family tradition says that a man with your surname who lived two hundred years ago is your great-great grandfather you will need to prove or disprove the relationship. If tradition is correct it can be proven on a pedigree chart or a descendancy chart. Beginning with you as no.1 on a pedigree chart you would work your way straight back on your direct line and your great-great grandfather would appear as an ancestor in the fifth generation.

Conversely, your "traditional" great-great grandfather (the one you're trying to prove) would be no. 1 on a descendancy chart. Descendancy charts most often run vertically with the no.1 spot at the top of the page. Each male child would be a direct descendant of no.1 and in turn would be the patriarch of new lines of grandchildren. This would be repeated (and multiplied) until the fifth generation is reached (yours). In theory, many lines would have to be researched to see if you appeared five generations down in any of them.

I have a special edition of "The Illustrated London News" which celebrated the coronation of King George VI (the present Queen's father) and shows the significance of descendancy charts in monarchies. It's a substantial A3 (15"x11") soft cover book containing 72 pages. The cover reads:

THE

ILLUSTRATED

LONDON NEWS

(King George VI portrait)

CORONATION

RECORD NUMBER

1937

On page 17 is an elaborate full color descendancy chart from Egbert (reigned 802-839) to King George VI (reigned 1936-1952). At the bottom of the page is its title:

The descent of King George VI: A genealogical table

Of the Kings and Queens of England.

It's extremely interesting, but as is the case with most descendancy charts, it is not easy to read. "The Genealogical Table of the Kings and Queens of England" illustrates the perspective of genealogical time. Egbert, whom they show as England's first King, was crowned nine hundred and eighty-eight years before America's first President was inaugurated!

While on pedigree charts, I have reservations about the newer ones being used today. The most accessible of the older ones were LDS and were typically five generations on legal-size paper and could be found at any LDS branch genealogy library. They were in use for almost forty years. The new LDS forms are four generations on letter-size paper, but to achieve this, they've done away with an important visual display (or perspective). It's easy to separate (or visualize) generations displayed in vertical columns, but in order to display four generations on the new sheets, they've crammed the first two generations into the left-hand column, destroying the concept of a column for each generation. There have been several new versions of the letter-size chart and I have found each one less serviceable as "working charts" than the previous. Additions on the 1987 charts include two generations in the left column, Each successive form seems "busier" and the names (the most important items on the charts) seem lost in all of the detail (clutter). The change to letter-size took place between 1980 and 1987. I have seen members' manuals from those two years, but none in between. The 1980 manual uses the legal-size charts and the 1987 manual uses the letter-size charts. I still use the old five-generation format. For those of you who haven't seen it, try it.

I like analogies. Oddly, I can find a certain parallelism between the actual work of genealogy and geology. In each the approach may take two forms–the study of individual family lines (local geology), or the construction of larger charts of collective pedigrees (regional or basin-wide geology). Pedigree charts are not unlike maps (they are the roadmaps that give direction to the work), and working with the larger charts (10-15 generations) gives a glimpse of the extent of the project. I find these large charts to be quite similar to regional maps (less detail but great for the big picture). They tell where all those smaller charts are headed, which sections need more work, and give a quick look at where we came from. I find the smaller charts similar to prospecting in a particular (subsurface) stream or distributary, and the large charts equivalent to giving one a look at the entire delta.

The use of Google Maps would be a further analogy. As you "zoom in and out" you get a local or regional picture. Having "zoomed in" your reaction could be "this is what I'm looking for, but where am I?". A reaction after "zooming out" could be "that's my region, but where is what I'm looking for?". I think it's interesting that working in all three (and diverse) areas lends itself to a similar approach. The genealogy and geology research is "hands-on" and should bring to mind the importance of having work areas that are suitable to "spreading out" the work. Having the small (detail) and large (extended) charts in front of you allows you to "toggle" your eyes from one scale to another.

The large pedigree charts reveal what genealogy really is (which few recognize at the outset) and illustrate just how broad the scope of serious genealogy can become. It's a work that can never be finished, and it's best to realize that aspect early on, rather than after fifty years of work. A good amount can be accomplished, but it must be broken down into manageable phases (how to do it is part of the fun and appeal). It isn't the purpose here to delve into techniques, but I must mention the first and foremost basic rule of genealogical research–always work backwards!

A look at the occurrence of surnames in the earliest days of our country gives an interesting perspective of its makeup. The first census of the United States was taken in 1790 (one year after George Washington was inaugurated President in New York City). In 1890 the Census Bureau issued a volume entitled "A Century of Population Growth". Its purpose was to preserve the records of the 1790 census (which had begun to deteriorate), and the statistics it contains should be of interest to genealogists.

In September 1909 Josiah Morrow, writing historical articles for "The Western Star" (an Ohio newspaper) pulled out some fascinating summaries regarding surnames. The tabulated schedules showed 27,337 different surnames in 1790. The 1790 schedules of New Jersey, Delaware, and Georgia were missing and only half of those for Virginia were obtainable. It was estimated that the total number of surnames for the entire country didn't exceed 30,000. Nearly half of that number was found in Pennsylvania which had nearly twice as many different names as any other state. It's thought to be due to the large proportion of Germans in the state.

The demographics might be surprising. Of the 27,337 surnames in the United States, only one family was reported for 11,934 of them. Although the number of names represented by a single family was large, the number of names represented by a single person was very small, being only 720! (a testimony of the importance of marriage in those days). There were less than 500 surnames that reported as many as 1000 persons. The numbers of persons bearing the most common surnames in 1790 were Smith (33,245), Brown (19,175), Davis (14,300), Jones (14.300), Johnson (14,001), Clark (13,766), Williams (12,717), Miller (12,694), and Wilson (9,797).

I'll end this chapter on perspectives with a favorite quote: "Everyman is an omnibus in which his ancestors ride" (Oliver Wendell Holmes, 1809-1894). It's a thought worthy of reflection any time, but particularly pertinent when we're working on our genealogy.

Before You Begin (or Continue)

One of the first things I had to learn before I began genealogy was that our ancestors didn't have to be famous to leave their footprints in time. I had hesitated for some time because the genealogy articles in magazines and the bound genealogies in libraries were mostly about famous or noteworthy people and families. I was finally encouraged by a friend in New York to go with him to the genealogy division of the New York City Public Library in Manhattan. That Saturday afternoon visit (and subsequent ones) opened up a new world of opportunity and resources that could be used to track down my ancestors.

Famous or no, I discovered that there is a long list of public and ecclesiastical records on which my family (past and present) could appear. I certainly started in an optimum setting since the first genealogical facilities, collections, and librarians I was exposed to must have been among the best in the country. The collections covering the Northeast and New York were extensive as were those of some European countries, especially Germany (I have some German lines). With help from my mentor and the librarians, I was introduced to an array of records in which my ancestors might appear (yours will be there too).

The sources to be searched in each of the families on our pedigree charts include vital statistics records (births, marriages, and deaths), census enumerator sheets, wills, obituaries, church (parish) registers, genealogical societies, family correspondence, local histories, phone books, old city directories, gazetteers, published books ("Encyclopedia of Quaker Genealogy" etc.), ships' passengers lists, military records, patriotic societies, family bibles, and family (surname) forums on the web, etc. Depending on where you are in your research, and where your localities are, you will be adding or subtracting from the list. Either way, the list addresses the initial feelings that many of us had (that we won't be able to find our ancestors because they weren't famous).

The very first step in a new genealogy program is the survey. That a survey should be made is obvious, but it's also important. The survey should be wide-ranging and should reveal what has already been done by you and others. Its purpose is to avoid duplication as well as gather information. There are several sides to a survey. People tend to forget that your genealogy begins with you. Your first locality (and localities are very important) is your home. You will be surprised that some of the very types of clues you are looking for in your search for ancestors are found at your fingertips and (similarly) they also identify your family and its members. Other prime areas might be offices and safe deposit boxes.

An obvious reason for the survey is to search for any previous genealogy that you or your family members have done. This involves reaching out to other branches of the family. Make copies of anything with genealogical implications and put it into a genealogy file (a word soon to become plural).

Another side of your survey also involves extended family, but is more specific to a particular group, the older family members (whether you've worked your way back to them or not). This is an exception to the rule of always working backwards. This is a group that may be gone when you've worked back, and you will have missed the opportunity to learn from them. At these early stages of your research you should be working at both ends of the ladder (pedigree chart), with you at the bottom rung and your older living relatives at the top.

Seemingly simple or silly things should not be ignored. (often, beginnings seem that way). In the early 1960's I was on a business trip to Kansas where I was studying an oil field from files at the Kansas State Geological Survey. I had been wanting to start on an exercise program and decided that I could begin one in the evenings if I could find a good manual. I settled on one used by the Royal Canadian Air Force (R.C.A.F.) that I had picked up at a local magazine shop.

There were ten exercises that were to be done each day. After three days at each level the number was to be doubled. The manual instructed the servicemen to strictly adhere to the routine and not be tempted to skip ahead. I opened up to page one only to find that I was to do one push-up, one jumping jack, one sit-up, touch my toes once, etc. It took about a minute (I'm supposed to do three days of this?). I thought it was silly but I followed through with it. I remember the fitness maintenance level to have been in the forties for each exercise and when I reached the recommended level I was glad I hadn't tried to skip ahead!

The point of the story is to remind you that gathering and copying papers and other items from around your home may seem silly but it isn't. It's an early and useful phase of your survey. Don't deviate from the plan and keep making those copies.

The basic unit of genealogical research is the family and your files should be broken down by family names (surnames). The accepted way for recording individual families is by family group sheets and as your research progresses the number of family group sheets in your surname files will build. Two additional tools that will help you sort out the family group sheets are time lines and pedigree charts.

Pedigree charts are essential. They are the road maps of family lines. Their most important aspect is that they are visual. They greatly eliminate the necessity of thumbing through group sheets in search of a particular family or generation. And, having found a family or generation, the pedigree chart nicely lays out its position on the branches of your family tree.

Pedigree charts come in many formats, the 8 ½ x 11 four-generation charts being the most common. When you look at a blank four-generation pedigree chart, and place it into context with what you're embarking on, it looks easy. It isn't. The four generations will be represented by you (and your spouse), your parents, your grandparents and your great-grandparents, The corresponding family group sheets will show you as a parent and child, your parents as parents and children, your grandparents as parents and children, and your great-grandparents as parents. Finding and dating events in the lives of this group can be more difficult than you might think.

Sixty years ago there were far fewer pedigree charts available and I still use (and prefer) the LDS 8 ½ x 14 (legal size) five-generation charts. The fifth generation column can be folded over easily to fit the chart into a normal size file folder. The scale is a good one for "working" charts to be shuffled and moved around with family group sheets. You can have a separate file for pedigree charts and/or include charts in the surname family files. The 8 ½ x 14 charts are available online from genealogy supplies stores but may be subject to copyright. Because pedigree charts are major building blocks of your genealogy there are further references to them elsewhere in the book. In one of the sections I refer to my genealogy "bible" as being an 8-generation pedigree chart (23 x 19) that was begun in 1950. It's still a work in progress.

Genealogy has a companion word– details. The two words are inseparable. In the book there's been a fair spectrum of topics discussed about what's involved in the work, along with a good look at the history of genealogy during the last sixty years (and what's gone on around it). If you've gotten this far in the book you will have recognized that there has been an emphasis on the research (or "working side") of genealogy. Within this area there have been further discussions on how to do the work, where to do the work, and what charts and forms to use. Most topics have been on the work side and not on the display side.

In most vocations and avocations (jobs and hobbies) involving investigation and research there are three basic phases: the gathering of information (data), the arranging and putting together of the information, and the analysis of the information. It's in the second phase that the how and where (major themes in the book) come into play, and I've gone to some extent to explore both. In writing about things that many people haven't seen or experienced it's often difficult to explain or find an example. Since writing earlier sections of the book I've uncovered more easily accessible examples of the "hands-on" workplace in addition to more references on pedigree charts. Of the (considerable) "situation room" examples in chapter four, the newest "find" is the best and it thoroughly demonstrates the theme.

There is a fantasy romantic comedy movie entitled "13 Going on 30" (2004) in which a 13 year-old girl is granted her wish to be 30 ("wishing dust"). It's not unlike Tom Hanks' well-known movie "Big". Jenna (that's her name) finds herself as one of the editors of her favorite fashion magazine ("Poise"). Important scenes in the movie show Jenna working up an idea for a future issue of "Poise", drawing upon her high school yearbook as a theme. All of the elements are there of my genealogy and geology analogies of chapter four.

There was a strong sense of familiarity as I looked at her office. It was a large "hands-on" office (not a computer in sight), with a large wallboard on one wall (cork or magnetic), covered with many clips and photos (reminiscent of my wallboards holding structural and stratigraphic cross-sections). Her main workspace is a quite long table (or desk) where she goes through magazines, folders, and over-size covers and clips, placing annotated "Post-its" on pages she wants to go back to (analogous to seven foot drafting tables, electric well surveys, and well completion cards).

We see a portable whiteboard being used in her presentation to the editorial board. Another scene is a clever one in the hall from which we can see into Jenna's office where she's on the floor arranging proofs from her photo shoot (didn't I mention a living room floor as a good place for spreading out "hands-on" genealogy?). The movie was a good reminder that there are still fields today where "hands-on" is the norm. It also reaffirms my belief that genealogy is one of those activities that requires the opportunity to be "spread out" beyond the screen of a computer.

The word "chart" is one of the many English words which can be used as nouns (mostly) or as verbs ("let's chart it up and see what it looks like"). Pedigree charts are a very important (and basic) part of genealogy. I find that in the "putting the pieces together" stage they are often referred to. I'm an advocate for clean charts that bring out the names and unmistakably connect them to others in their line. There are many available charts that lose sight of a chart's main purpose and are just "too much". There are too many charts that miss the point.

There are two reasons why I favor the clean, easily read type of chart. The "Practical Genealogist" and its contents primarily address "working" charts and forms. Even basic forms evolve, and because pedigree charts are very good for research, we should keep up with what's available. Secondly, I take the word literally and maintain that a chart is a chart and not a document. A pedigree chart is a particular way to concisely present data and needn't contain a "file" under each name. Family group sheets do that. I consider a good pedigree chart to be a "graphic", containing the familiar "tuning fork" pattern as it goes from child to parents and from generation to generation. The most common format is horizontal with the number 1 name (the first generation) on the left. I have seen vertical charts with the first generation at the bottom (that also works).

Genealogy forms evolve, and pedigree charts have been excellent for following the changes. Depending on your purposes and preferences the changes haven't all been good. Because the LDS are leaders in the field and quite visible, a look at their charts is useful. They've changed considerably through the years, apparently to accommodate new technology. I have referred several times to the legal-size five-generation charts that I favor. They were discontinued in 1969 and were replaced (after decades of use) by the letter-size four-generation charts found in later manuals for members. The 1987 version illustrates the movement away from a "hands-on" format to a technological format. It's "busy" by comparison and tends to devalue important data.

Thirty-three lines have been added to the new chart: six "ordinance blocks" under each name comprising sixteen new lines, eleven lines for a blocks key, three vertical sidebars (entry instructions), and eight new marriage lines for "place" under the "mother" fields.

The latest of the letter-size charts came out in the 2009 Member's Guide. These latest are the furthest removed from the clean five-generation charts of the early "journey" years. They have the look of a document as opposed to a chart and it takes some doing to see the typical elements of a chart. The blocks key has been removed from the upper left and has been replaced by three triple-space lines of tying-in with other charts. The key to the blocks and other instructions take up a half page on the reverse. The additional space is accounted for by the expansion of the entry spaces under the names throughout the charts. All of the entries are now on lines, which add eighty lines to the page. A seventh ordinance block is added throughout. It's a very "busy" page.

The first two generations remain in the left-hand column. The lower entry lines infringe on the names, making them appear almost "boxed" (and hard to see). The horizontal aspect of a traditional pedigree chart yields to a "document-like" vertical aspect. Most disconcerting is that the placement of the branches of the family tree is asymmetrical in order to fit everything in. The largest offset is where the names of the numbers 4 and 5 couple intersect the number 2 name's line nearly an inch below the symmetrical norm. In the early years, LDS charts were more "universal" and were available to the general public at all branch genealogy libraries. As time went by, the pedigree charts have transitioned to the extent that they are "weighted" for use by Church members. The progression of these LDS charts from simple to complex isn't unique but is quite common among genealogical houses. Many have made the transition from easily readable "graphics" to charts that need to be scrutinized.

The scope and focus of your genealogy project is a personal decision. If, like most of us, you are looking for your beginnings (your "roots") you will concentrate on the lines of your direct ancestors (progenitors), and bypass your collateral lines in your early work. Collateral lines include those of your aunts, uncles, and cousins. If you are putting together a particular section in the genealogy of your family or are doing a descendancy project, you should adapt your approach to its purpose.

Genealogical sources have been broken down into classes from the most reliable to document an event. The event may involve an individual (birth, marriage, death) or a family (immigration date, emigration date, or the buying of a house, or the burning of a mortgage). It is generally accepted that there are three categories- primary, secondary, and tertiary. It may be easier to remember them as first class, second class, and third class, since we're used to using those terms to designate quality. An example of a primary source is a record of an event that was made at the time (or very close to the time) of an event. It could have been made by a witness to the event or a clerk or pastor who is responsible for keeping civil or ecclesiastical records.

Secondary sources are records (or documents) which were not made at the time of an event. A family bible can be either. If an entry is made at the time of a birth or marriage, it is a primary source. If written in some time later, it's a secondary source. A good example of a tertiary source is the bibliography, which lists places where primary or secondary sources may be found. There are many specific sources in each category. As you get into the work you will learn to differentiate between sources and it will benefit you in your research.

There is so much software available that the subject is well beyond the scope of this book. When I was looking for software (many years ago) I brought home several versions that had received good reviews and (after working with them) they all went back. I have always evaluated genealogy programs and software by pedigree charts (I rely on them heavily while doing the work). When I'm working on a line I look for movement and not elaboration. A few of the prominent software sources are Ancestry.com, Reunion.com, and MyTrees.com. The straight-forward PAF 2.3.1 (for the Mac) and the PAF 5.0 format (for Windows) are no longer supported by the LDS Church but should still be available.

There are dozens of pedigree charts to choose from though some don't fit the name. Pictures by each name seem to be a favorite feature but don't make for good "working" charts. A fully leafed-out tree with ancestral pictures on the branches (like apples on a tree), but no further details, is available. Standard charts with "boxed" names are popular but the boxes take your eyes off of the names. Some charts have excessive entries under the early generations such as "occupation" and "hobbies". I've seen listings for "DNA" pedigree charts. The latter is also a tool used by geneticists. There are charts in the shape of a fan (a half-circle). There are circular charts that somewhat resemble the Mayan calendar at a distance. There are many choices and from among them you have a very good chance of finding one that suits you.

It's time to wrap up. I've covered some essentials but not all of them. By the tone of the book, you will probably have an opinion on the direction I would take on the essentials not covered. There's a lot of "caveat emptor" in the book but it should be useful as a general guide. It's been all about doing and less about show. It's been about the useful above the elaborate, the obvious above the complex, and the direct above the obscure. It's been about the treatment you give your findings.

Genealogy is ancient (by thousands of years). Its present status and interpretation is strongly influenced by being overlain by the new technology. In my experience, it doesn't always fit.

This book is a point of view, but it's a point of view that works.

www.ingramcontent.com/pod-product-compliance
Lightning Source LLC
Chambersburg PA
CBHW070546290526
45790CB00002B/598